# SEVEN STEPS TO
# Separating
# Difference
# FROM
# Disability

# SEVEN STEPS TO
# Separating
# Difference
## FROM
# Disability

## Catherine Collier

CORWIN
A SAGE Company

*For information:*

Corwin
A SAGE Company
2455 Teller Road
Thousand Oaks, California 91320
(800) 233-9936
Fax: (800) 417-2466
www.corwin.com

SAGE India Pvt. Ltd.
B 1/I 1 Mohan Cooperative Industrial Area
Mathura Road, New Delhi 110 044
India

SAGE Ltd.
1 Oliver's Yard
55 City Road
London EC1Y 1SP
United Kingdom

SAGE Asia-Pacific Pte. Ltd.
33 Pekin Street #02-01
Far East Square
Singapore 048763

Printed in the United States of America

*Library of Congress Cataloging-in-Publication Data*

Collier, Catherine.
Seven steps to separating difference from disability / Catherine Collier.
    p. cm.
Includes bibliographical references.
ISBN 978-1-4129-7160-7 (pbk.)

    1. Linguistic minorities—Education—United States. 2. Learning disabilities—Diagnosis—United States. 3. English language—Study and teaching—United States—Foreign speakers. I. Title.

LC3731.C618 2011
371.829—dc22                               2010020318

This book is printed on acid-free paper.

15  16  17  18  19  10  9  8  7  6  5  4  3

| | |
|---|---|
| *Acquisitions Editor:* | Jessica Allan |
| *Associate Editor:* | Joanna Coelho |
| *Editorial Assistant:* | Allison Scott |
| *Production Editor:* | Amy Schroller |
| *Copy Editor:* | Jenifer Dill |
| *Typesetter:* | C&M Digitals (P) Ltd. |
| *Proofreader:* | Ellen Howard |
| *Indexer:* | Sheila Bodell |
| *Cover Designer:* | Rose Storey |

# Contents

# Acknowledgments

Corwin gratefully acknowledges the contributions of the following reviewers:

Joyce Bergin
Professor and Assistant Dean
College of Education
Armstrong Atlantic State
    University
Savannah, GA

Margarete Couture
Principal
South Seneca Central School
    District
Interlaken, NY

Dawne Dragonetti
Special Education Teacher and
    Instructional Coach
Nashoba Regional School District
Stow, MA

Kay Kuenzl-Stenerson
Literacy Coach
Merrill Middle School
Oshkosh, WI

Karen Kozy-Landress
Speech/Language Pathologist
Brevard County Schools
Merritt Island, FL

Jacie Maslyk
Principal
Crafton Elementary School
Pittsburgh, PA

Judith A. Rogers
K–5 Mathematics Specialist
Tucson Unified School District
Tucson, AZ

Rachel L. Skinkis
Current Grade 6 Teacher/Former
    ELL Teacher
School District of New Holstein
Little Chute, WI

# About the Author

Photograph by George
C. Anderson

**Catherine Collier** has more than 45 years of experience in equity, cross-cultural, bilingual, and special education, beginning with voter registration in 1964. She completed her PhD with research into the referral of Latino/Hispanic students to special education programs. For eight years, she was a classroom teacher, resource room teacher, and diagnostician for the Bureau of Indian Affairs in Arizona and Alaska. She established and directed the Chinle Valley School, *Dine Bitsiis Baa Aha Yaa,* serving special needs clients and their families for the Navajo Nation. She was the director of a teacher-training program for the University of Alaska for seven years, preparing Yup'ik Eskimo, *Ikayurikiit Unatet,* paraprofessionals for certification as bilingual preschool, elementary, and special educators. For eight years, Dr. Collier worked with the BUENO Center for Multicultural Education, Research, and Evaluation at the University of Colorado, Boulder, where she created and directed the Bilingual Special Education Curriculum/Training project (BISECT), a nationally recognized effort. She was the Director of Resource and Program Development for the American Indian Science and Engineering Society, as well as being a Sequoyah Fellow.

Dr. Collier is the author of several books and articles on cross-cultural and multilingual special education. She is active in social justice activities for culturally and linguistically diverse learners and families. She works extensively with school districts on professional and program development for at-risk diverse learners. Dr. Collier provides technical assistance to university, local, and state departments of education regarding programs that serve at-risk cognitively, culturally, and linguistically diverse learners.

She is the director of the national professional development project Curriculum Integration for Responsive, CrossCultural, Language-Based Education (CIRCLE) at Western Washington University. She is the principal developer of the screening and software program "Acculturation Quick Screen" and many assessment and intervention instruments and materials. Her most recent publications include a chapter on acculturation in the *Multicultural Handbook for School Psychologists,* a book titled *Response to Intervention for Diverse Learners,* and this text, *Seven Steps to Separating Difference From Disability.*

# Introduction

## *Reaching Culturally and Linguistically Diverse Students*

In the United States, the last few decades have seen an increase in schools' efforts to meet all students' educational needs. One category of needs that has received considerable focus is the effective diagnosis and support of students with disabilities. Many students are benefiting from this additional attention placed on special education services; however, culturally and linguistically diverse (CLD) students' needs are often left unmet by the interventions implemented in school districts throughout the United States (Hoover, Baca, & Klingner, 2007). In some instances, students' cultural and linguistic differences are mistaken for learning or behavioral disabilities. In other instances, these cultural and linguistic differences actually mask a student's disability. Despite significant advances in the understanding of effective teaching practices for CLD students, including limited English proficient (LEP) and English language learners (ELL), the transfer of research to practice remains scant (Bui, Simpson, & Alvarado, 2007).

One of the primary proponents for the effective diagnosis and support of students with disabilities is the 2004 reauthorization of the Individuals with Disabilities Education Act. The reauthorized IDEA leads states away from discrepancy and checklist screening and guides them to employ a more effective method to identify specific learning and behavior disabilities (Bradley, Danielson, & Doolittle, 2005). As a result of this legislation, most states have begun to implement intervention models involving problem solving with progress monitoring.

## PROBLEM SOLVING

Two of the most popular models of problem solving with progress monitoring are response to intervention (RTI) and response to instruction and intervention (RTII). Although not mandated, most districts are now using some variation of RTI and RTII models to identify and address learning and behavior problems.

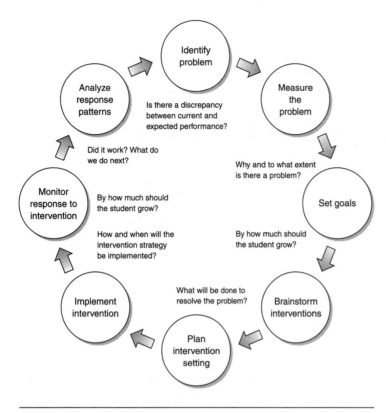

**Figure 1**   Problem Solving and Monitoring Process

In current instructional intervention models, such as RTI and RTII, an instruction and intervention implementation team composed of instructional personnel, rather than specialists, forms the body of educators responsible for working with the target student. Their focus is on problem solving and instruction, not on formal evaluation—though most of the models include a range of progress monitoring in their implementation (see Figure 1). The team meets for differing lengths of time, depending on what intensity of instructional intervention they are using for the target student. At the beginning stage of services, most of the interventions occur within the general education classroom. The stages of instruction and intervention in RTI or RTII models are commonly referred to as *tiers*, representing the layers of variation in intensity. RTI and RTII models usually have three or four tiers.

At each stage, or tier, the team assists the classroom teacher with differentiation of instruction and monitoring of student progress as part of the problem solving process. At the first tier for culturally and linguistically diverse learners, the focus is on building a foundation for learning, and differentiation occurs within the core curriculum program and may include bilingual assistance or instruction. At the second tier, there is usually more focus and intensity of implementation (e.g., small groups or pairing of the target student with peers for short specific instruction) and more progress monitoring of target CLD students in comparison with their CLD peers. At the third tier, the team assists with strategic intensive intervention and monitoring over a fixed period of time, typically six to eight weeks and no longer than twelve. There is an intensive focus at this level for CLD students to comprehensively document the degree to which the students' language and culture are contributing to their learning or behavior problems.

Although CLD students can be referred for special education at any point it is determined that their learning and behavior problems are not due to cultural or linguistic differences and are beyond the capacity of general education personnel alone, in problem-solving models such as RTI and RTII, this usually does not occur until the team has completed two or three tiers of strategic instructional intervention. At the end of this period, the team makes a decision about whether to proceed with a formal referral to an evaluation team or whether the interventions have resolved the learning and behavior problems seen in the student. The team may decide a formal referral is necessary if they have seen no evidence of a successful, positive response to selected problem-focused interventions, if the level and intensity of intervention necessary for the student to succeed are not sustainable within the general education program, or if there are still a number of unanswered questions about the student at the end of these tiered instructional intervention periods. The team may decide a formal referral is not warranted if they have seen considerable improvement in response to the focused interventions or if they have determined that social, cultural, linguistic, or socioeconomic issues are the primary factors contributing to the student's learning or behavior problems.

RTI and RTII problem solving with progress monitoring models are frequently depicted by a triangle, with levels or tiers indicated within the shape, such as that shown in Figure 2.

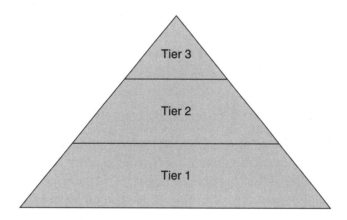

**Figure 2**   Three Tier Problem Solving Triangle

Research on the efficacy of intervention models such as RTI and RTII for culturally and linguistically diverse learners is sparse and inconsistent. Nevertheless, RTI and RTII programs have been used to answer the common CLD question: Is this learning and behavior problem due to an undiagnosed disability, or is it due to the student's limited English proficiency or cultural differences? RTI/RTII and problem solving models for CLD students must address more than just academic performance in reading and mathematics. When using RTI and RTII problem solving and progress monitoring with CLD students, especially nonnative English speakers and those with limited English proficiency, complex learning and behavior issues must be addressed as well. Addressing these concerns for culturally and linguistically diverse students can be very challenging in today's schools, and many schools struggle to find the personnel and resources to address them appropriately (Bui et al., 2007).

One response to this challenging situation is an intervention model developed by the author that uses RTI and RTII methodology as its foundation but also addresses and monitors the process of facilitating resiliency, maintaining effective instruction, and implementing the intensive interventions that are critical in the instruction of and intervention for culturally and linguistically diverse learners. This process is called the Pyramid of Resiliency, Instruction, Strategies, Intervention, and Monitoring (PRISIM; see Figure 3). There are seven steps to the dynamic PRISIM process of separating difference from disability to assure that diverse students with special needs are not disproportionately identified (either under or over) for special services and to ensure that all students with special needs have those needs met in the most appropriate manner.

## Step 1. Building and Sustaining a Foundation for Learning

- Gathering information about incoming students to determine their diverse needs and strengths. Utilizing this information to connect students and their families to available resources in the community.
- Using the information and prescreening to place students in an appropriate initial instructional environment.
- Assisting the student's family's access to resources to facilitate their supporting and assisting of the CLD student in the school.

## Step 2. Establishing and Supporting Resiliency

- Gathering information about students' educational resiliency (i.e., what skills and strengths the diverse students bring with them that will facilitate achieving to the best of their ability).
- Providing differentiated learning support to all learners that promotes and sustains resiliency in a developmentally appropriate manner.
- Monitoring the effectiveness of these strategies and instructions by a problem solving with progress monitoring approach (e.g., RTI or RTII).
- In programs using the tiered RTI or RTII model, this step coincides with Tier 1.

## Step 3. Instructional Intervention and Differentiated Instruction

- Screening to determine what diverse factors contribute significantly to emerging learning and behavior problems in order to identify learning and behavioral strategies that may effectively resolve these problems.
- Providing differentiated learning support and instruction to students who have specific learning and behavior needs.
- In programs using the tiered RTI or RTII model, this step coincides with Tier 1 and Tier 2

## Step 4. Intensive Intervention and Progress Monitoring

- Designing and implementing an intensive instructional intervention plan with specifically targeted progress monitoring to determine the student's response to intervention.

- Implementing a sequence of specific individualized interventions to identify the capacity of a CLD learner to participate effectively in your school's programs.
- Identifying specific areas of concern in the CLD student's response to intervention that warrant further evaluation and monitoring.
- In programs using the tiered RTI or RTII model, this step coincides with Tier 3.

## Step 5. Resolution or Referral

- Reviewing and analyzing the information gathered during the progress monitoring part of the problem solving process to determine if the student requires additional screening and assessment (formal referral) or if sufficient progress has been documented to take the student out of the intensive individualized intervention and place them back in less intensive instructional settings similar to Step 2 or Step 3 settings.
- In programs using the tiered RTI or RTII model, this step coincides with the decision to stop Tier 3 interventions and move on to Tier 4.
- The intervention team reviews all instruction and intervention up to this point and makes data-based decisions on whether to continue intensive individualized interventions, to return the student to a less intensive group intervention setting, or to begin a formal evaluation and assessment procedure.

## Step 6. Integrated Services

- Determining a student's special individualized instructional needs and outlining a monitoring and service plan.
- If special education and related services are appropriate, the student is served in a program that meets the student's unique instructional needs and an individualized plan of instruction or individual educational plan (IEP) is developed. The IEP must include language and culture accommodations that reflect the interaction of the student's unique and special needs, as well as the student's specific language, acculturation, and culture needs.
- In programs using the tiered RTI or RTII model, this step is sometimes incorporated into Tier 4.

## Step 7. Maintaining and Sustaining Programs Serving CLDE Students

- Verifying qualifications of bilingual personnel and paraprofessionals involved in the comprehensive service structure for culturally and linguistically diverse exceptional (CLDE) students, as described under current US federal law.
- Continuous monitoring and dynamic service placement across all tiers.
- Building and sustaining the most effective elements of such problem solving with progress monitoring programs across all levels of instruction.

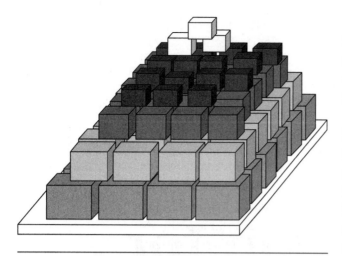

**Figure 3**    Pyramid of Resiliency, Instruction, Strategies, Intervention, and Monitoring

In the PRISIM pyramid of success model, based on problem solving with progress monitoring, the tiered interventions and prevention strategies are extensive within each layer of learning-strategy building blocks.

A pyramid shape made up of many building blocks and several layers illustrates the PRISIM pyramid problem solving model. The pyramid of interventions is built from many specific strategy blocks. Each block represents a specific strategy or approach, which may or may not be effective for an individual student. As various intervention and prevention approaches are used with individual students, they fill in that particular tier of the pyramid. The intensity of intervention and instruction increases as students advance from one tier to the next. Moreover, as the intensity of services increases, the number of students served at each tier decreases and, thus, the number of strategies employed at each progressive tier also decreases. This is shown by the decreasing number of blocks going up the pyramid. In some school districts, students will be moved upward until their needs are met and then moved back down to a lower tier to solidify the problem resolution. Not all students return entirely to Tier 1; some may need to continue on Tier 2 differentiation their entire school career.

Problem solving and process monitoring models such as RTI or RTII seek to move emphasis away from formal evaluations in order to more effectively identify students' specific learning and behavior disabilities. Unfortunately, as most versions of the models currently employed by school districts were developed for native English-speaking students, CLD students continue to be frequently misdiagnosed and their needs are left unmet (Hoover et al., 2007). For culturally and linguistically diverse students, problem-solving models must address more than academic performance in reading and mathematics, which is the focus of many RTI and RTII models. The PRISIM model demonstrates one way RTI/RTII processes can be modified and expanded when using problem solving and progress monitoring to separate difference from disability for CLD, ELL, and LEP students (Collier, 2008b).

# Building and Sustaining a Foundation for Learning 1

**PRISIM Step 1. Building and Sustaining a Foundation for Learning**

*Gathering information about incoming students to determine their diverse needs and strengths. Utilizing this information to connect students and their families to available resources in the community. Using the information and prescreening to place students in an appropriate initial instructional environment. Assisting the student's family's access to resources to facilitate their supporting and assisting of the CLD student in the school.*

**A** pyramid is only as strong as its foundation, and in the case of the PRISIM pyramid, the more comprehensive and complete the information gathering, teacher preparation, curricula, and system support can be, the stronger and more effective the instructional program of the school will be. The foundation of personnel, system, curricula, and comprehensive data provides a solid base upon which the building blocks of learning are firmly established. Each block represents a cluster of strategies, content, and settings that may be differentiated for specific strengths and/or needs of learners.

Many elements of the foundation for learning are not immediately accessible to school systems but, rather, are part of community services, agencies, religious organizations, or other institutions within the state or community. The function of

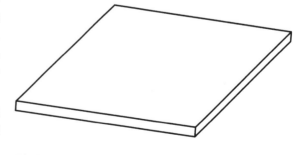

**Figure 4** Building a Foundation for the PRISIM Pyramid

these services for culturally and linguistically diverse (CLD) children should be to promote and sustain the following:

- Access to safety, food, clothing, and shelter
- Quality preparation of effective education professionals and support staff
- Adequacy of school facilities and resources
- Consistent use of culturally and linguistically responsive evidence-based practices
- Supportive, responsive relationships
- Other effective practices and procedures

Building an accurate and instructionally meaningful set of learning approaches begins when a student from a linguistically or culturally diverse background enrolls in your school district or school. Thus, the capacity to collect and use appropriate and comprehensive data at enrollment must be established and sustained in your school district. Students who have a primary or home language other than English (PHLOTE) are identified at the intake point to assess their need for second language and acculturation assistance. The identification of PHLOTE students occurs as part of the enrollment process or during a special session prior to the beginning of school at an intake center.

At registration or at an intake center, parents are provided with an enrollment form and should be given a home language survey or questioned about their home language and culture. The following are the types of questions that are typically asked:

1. Is a language other than English spoken in your home?

2. Do you speak another language in addition to English?

3. Does your child speak a language other than English?

4. Does your child speak another language in addition to English?

5. Has your child been schooled in a language other than English?

6. What language did your child speak before you enrolled him or her in school?

7. Do any adults in your home use a language other than English?

8. Do you want to receive school communications in a language other than English?

It is also useful to find out about the child's prior schooling and language learning experiences. Some districts have a single form that collects both sets of information. Preliminary identification as a PHLOTE student may be made at this time. If there is a positive PHLOTE identification, students are assessed for language proficiency and acculturation level. Whether or not the PHLOTE child is also an English language learner (ELL) or is a limited English proficient (LEP) speaker in need of English as a second language (ESL) or English language development (ELD) and would benefit from bilingual services and instruction is also determined at this time. The terms *limited English proficient*

(LEP) and *English language learner* (ELL) are used by the federal government and most states to identify those students who have insufficient English to succeed in English-only classrooms (Lessow-Hurley, 1991).

Language proficiency is usually assessed via a standardized instrument, and the scores are used to determine eligibility for services. At this point, it is best to assess the student's proficiency in both the home language and in English, as both sets of data are critical for service placement decisions. Using a process such as the Acculturation Quick Screen (AQS), school personnel should also assess the entering PHLOTE student's level of acculturation at this time. (See Figure 11 in Chapter 2 of this book or Collier, 2004a, for an example.) Making an acculturation or adaptation screen part of the intake process would provide a baseline for monitoring both the rate and level of adaptation, should incoming students later be identified as at-risk for learning or behavior problems.

Teachers and staff follow the same diagnostic procedures at both onsite school registrations and at an intake center. First, the school staff provides the parent with an enrollment form upon entering the school. Typically, these enrollment forms include a number of questions at the top of the form that ask what languages other than English are spoken in the home and whether the parent will need an interpreter. Personnel, usually the school secretary, go over these language and culture questions on the top of the enrollment form and hand a parent information form to those parents initially identified in this manner as potential PHLOTEs. In districts serving small populations, the parent information form about home language and culture may be given to every parent enrolling a child to avoid the chance of leaving out any population needing assistance with adaptation to the school. The secretarial and clerical staff at each building should include at least one person who is bilingual in the languages and knowledgeable about the cultures that are most common in the community. If the parent speaks a language that is not spoken by anyone on the school staff, the secretary arranges for an interpreter through the district or area resource center. After the parent completes the enrollment form and the parent information form, the secretary reviews the forms to ensure that the information is complete. If any parent leaves the questions regarding home language blank, the staff member asks the parent to complete those questions. An assigned staff member reviews the forms, separating them into two categories: (1) those whose home language is English and (2) those who speak a language other than English at home. School staff places copies of the PHLOTE student's enrollment and parent information forms in the individual's cumulative file, which will be maintained until the student graduates.

Education personnel maintain a list of all PHLOTE students at each school. After PHLOTE identification, specific ELL or LEP personnel are responsible for follow-up substantiation after enrollment through documented teacher observation, observations by other school personnel, and student interviews. This should include a language proficiency assessment and an AQS. Following is a list of questions districts should be able to answer when a student from a linguistically or culturally diverse background enrolls in one of their schools:

1.  Who receives the student and parents? What training do they have to prepare intake forms and provide information to CLD families about the school system? How are they trained to work effectively with diverse populations?

2. How are the student's language(s) and ethnicity or culture identified? If informal measures are used, how is proficiency determined?

3. If interpretation and translation are necessary, who provides this? What qualifications or training are required for translators?

4. What questions are the parents asked? How are responses quantified, and how is the information conveyed to program personnel?

5. What background information about the student is documented at the initial enrollment? How is this information used to determine service and classroom placement?

6. What criteria are used to determine eligibility for bilingual/ESL services? Who makes this determination, and how is the decision conveyed to school personnel?

In conclusion, a district must be sure that the personnel receiving the parents and students are competent in cross-cultural communication techniques and familiar with district policies and resources for PHLOTE and ELL/LEP students. There should be a procedure for accurately identifying the student's ethnicity, culture, and language(s), including languages used in the home by primary caregivers. A resource bank of qualified interpreters needs to be made available and should be on call in case they are needed. Enrollment information must be available in translation, if needed. Interpreters and translators should be trained in cross-cultural communication techniques and on all relevant intake forms and procedures. There must be a process to document and distribute relevant data about culture and language so that districts have clear criteria to establish eligibility for bilingual and ESL services. This foundation of information provides part of the structural base of the problem-solving pyramid. Additional foundation pieces are building blocks such as highly qualified education professionals effective with CLD and culturally and linguistically diverse exceptional (CLDE) students, appropriate and stimulating curricula that facilitate accelerated learning, and systems that encourage creative, physical, and cognitive growth for all students.

## OUR DIVERSE STUDENTS

The population of diverse students in the United States and Canada is increasing steadily, and it will continue to be a challenge to educators for many years. Culturally and linguistically diverse students include those from homes where languages other than English and dialects other than Standard English are spoken. They also include students from families of racial and ethnic backgrounds that differ from the majority population in the United States and Canada, such as African Americans and Quebecois, depending on the region.

CLD, LEP, and ELL students in schools include students from immigrant, refugee, and migrant families, as well as students from indigenous communities (also called First Nations, American Indian, or Native American). Approximately

60% of CLD, LEP, and ELL students in the United States speak Spanish at home, 20% speak an Asian language in the home, and 20% speak any one of 300 other languages or dialects in the home (Baca & Cervantes, 2003).

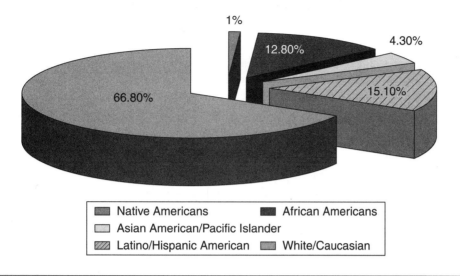

**Figure 5**   Ethnicity in the US Population (US Bureau of Census, 2005)

According to the 2005 US census (Figure 5), 33% of the US population at that time was non-Caucasian and by 2012, students of color are projected to account for 24% of the total school population, while 90% of teachers will be white females. There are six states and the District of Columbia where white students are the minority: California, Texas, Michigan, Hawaii, New Mexico, and Florida (Samuels, 2007).

Additional diversity factors for CLD students are poverty and other socio-economic conditions that impact families. Approximately 20% of the students in the average US classroom come from homes characterized by poverty or come from neighborhoods beset with inadequate health, social, or cultural services, low employment opportunities, crime, drugs, and gangs. Yet Bui, Simpson, and Alvardo (2007) noted that within the Latino population in the United States, which is projected to increase to 47 million by the year 2010, 39 out of 100 Latino children live in poverty and 37% of Latinos will not finish high school (Figure 6). Latino students are overrepresented in remedial programs, particularly for students with learning disabilities, and underrepresented in programs for gifted and talented students (Baca & Cervantes, 2003). Another minority group that is often overlooked regarding its CLD and CLDE status is African Americans. While African American students are proficient in English, many speak a dialect called African American English (AAE). They also come from backgrounds that differ racially and ethnically from the majority populations of the United States and Canada.

Among the diverse students mentioned in the preceding paragraphs are those who have special learning and behavior problems, some of which may be due to the presence of disabling conditions. There are currently approximately 600,000 disabled students between the ages of 5 and 12 who are from non-English language backgrounds in US public schools (Baca & Cervantes, 2003). Often, special education students with language or cultural differences do not have their language needs met, either through ESL instruction, ELL services, or other approaches. The Individuals with Disabilities Education Act (IDEA) requires that an Individual Education Plan (IEP) be developed for each student to comprehensively address the needs of the exceptional student and it includes guidelines about accommodations for culturally and linguistically diverse exceptional (CLDE) learners. The school district may not access such services, however, if it cannot meet the language and cultural needs of the exceptional student due to lack of resources or staff trained in bilingual special education. It is of paramount importance that these students are identified early and that their unique learning needs are addressed as effectively and comprehensively as possible. Some learning and behavior problems may be due to the students' different sociolinguistic and cultural backgrounds, their adjustment to a new sociocultural milieu, the presence of a disabling condition, or the combined effects of these situations.

The learning and behavior problems exhibited by diverse and at-risk students are often similar to the problems that elicit referrals for any students. These include lack of, or seriously deficient, academic achievement and social and classroom behavior that is disruptive to instruction, as well as other problems that are difficult for the teacher to handle in the general classroom setting without specific training. One major difference between CLD students and mainstream students who exhibit these behaviors lies in the interaction (or lack thereof) among cultural and sociolinguistic factors and a suspected disability (i.e., learning disability, mental impairment, emotional disturbance). The level of interaction of these various factors also influences decisions concerning the most effective intervention for resolution of the problem. US federal law requires that school districts demonstrate that they are doing everything possible to facilitate the effective participation of CLD students in their academic programs. Nevertheless, recent research shows that districts have steadily undercounted the rate at which students have left or dropped out of the instructional program altogether (Wallis, 2008).

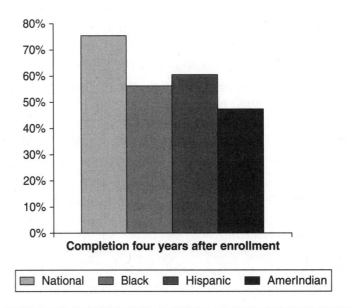

**Figure 6**   High School Completion Rate, 2005

Under the No Child Left Behind Act of 2002, districts must annually demonstrate that their LEP students are making specific English language proficiency and achievement gains. The US Office of Civil Rights conducts regular monitoring and investigative activities in school districts to assure that CLD and LEP students are able to participate effectively at or near peer level in all programs and content areas, including those at risk and those with special education needs. Students with primary or home languages other than English (PHLOTE), as well as CLDE and LEP students should have the same access to content instruction as their non-PHLOTE peers and the same assistance with learning and achievement as their non-LEP peers. LEP gifted students should have access to the same gifted services as non-LEP, LEP special education students to the same special education services, and so on. The key to all of this is separating difference from disability and using that information to develop appropriate instruction.

Identifying which students are PHLOTE and which are LEP has become more challenging for schools recently, as more linguistically diverse students come from mixed language homes. Figure 7 illustrates data from 2005 that show the number of LEP families where English is also used in the home. By the third generation, over 95% of LEP families use English in the home, in comparison to less than 8% of the first generation.

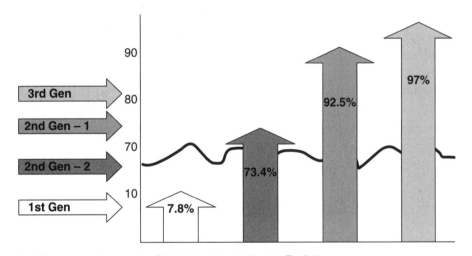

2nd Gen-1: one parent spoke English and one spoke non-English.
2nd Gen-2: both parents spoke non-English.

**Figure 7**    LEP Families Speaking English in the Home (Rumbaut, 2005).

The challenge to differentiating PHLOTE from LEP students has been further increased by the fact that more and more of the LEP students in our schools are native born and not immigrants or refugees. Figure 8 shows the proportion of LEP students in U.S. American schools who are native born versus foreign born in 2000. Most students in ELL programs in today's schools are second and third generation limited English proficient students who come to school with a mix of English and the home language, in varying levels of development.

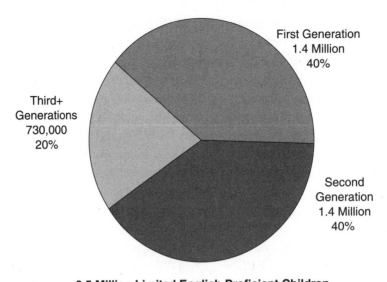

**3.5 Million Limited English Proficient Children**
(Ages 5–19, US Census 2000 Supplementary Survey)

**Figure 8**   Native Born LEP, 2000

An additional complication is in regard to regulations for the Individuals with Disabilities Education Act (IDEA). These regulations require that school personnel exclude culture, language, and socioeconomic disadvantage as factors in their at-risk students' learning and behavior problems before proceeding with special education placement decisions. Unfortunately, in CLD students, learning and behavior problems that seem to be indicative of a disabling condition may actually be the manifestation of cultural and sociolinguistic differences, or they may indicate problems related to a combination of cultural and linguistic factors and a disabling condition. When addressing these learning and behavior problems in diverse student populations, one must consider these possibilities and the legal requirements in working with CLD students.

In addition to gathering information about the learning and behavior problems of CLD students, assessment personnel should also gather relevant sociocultural information on those students. Analyzing such information prior to formal evaluation facilitates student placement and programming by demonstrating the extent to which sociocultural and language or dialect factors impact the learning and behavior problems of a CLD student. This consideration in the formal assessment process helps schools meet the legal requirements for assessment of CLD students.

Legislation has addressed the identification and assessment of culturally and linguistically diverse exceptional (CLDE) students for many years, and these cases have generated several legal guidelines. The cases of *Dyrcia S. et al. v. Board of Education of the City of New York et al.* (1979), *Larry P. v. Riles* (1979), and *José P. v. Ambach* (1979) are very significant because they address the cultural and sociolinguistic needs, as well as the special education needs, of CLDE students. Baca and Cervantes (2003) summarized pertinent recommendations resulting from these cases and other litigation, including the following:

1. Identification of students who need special education services must include the use of adequate bilingual resources.

2. Appropriate evaluation must include the establishment of school-based support teams to evaluate students in their own environment using a bilingual, nondiscriminatory evaluation process.

3. Appropriate programs in the least restrictive environment must include a comprehensive continuum of services with the provision of appropriate bilingual programs at each place on the continuum for students with limited English proficiency.

4. Due process and parental and student rights must include a native language version of a parents' rights booklet, which explains all of the due process rights of students and parents. Also included is the hiring of neighborhood workers to facilitate parental involvement in the evaluation and development of the individualized educational program (IEP).

5. Education personnel must conduct a language screening at the beginning of each school year to determine if the new students are exposed to or influenced by a language other than English.

6. If this initial language screening indicates the presence of a language other than English, school personnel must conduct an assessment of language dominance and proficiency.

7. School personnel must inform parents of all due process rights in their native or most proficient language. Schools must provide an interpreter at all meetings if parents cannot communicate effectively in English.

8. When analyzing evaluation data for placement decisions, education professionals must draw information from a variety of sources, including socioeconomic and cultural background and adaptive behavior.

9. Education professionals must develop an IEP that reflects the student's linguistic and cultural needs if it is determined that a CLD student is both disabled and has limited English proficiency.

Many of the provisions in the Improving Education Results for Children with Disabilities Act of 2004, which reformed the Individuals with Disabilities Education Act (IDEA), led to improved educational success for students with disabilities. The legislation furthered many of the trends seen in education in the past few years, such as increasing accountability for students with disabilities, ensuring the presence of highly qualified teachers in our classrooms, expanding the types of methods used to identify students with learning disabilities, and reducing litigation. Furthermore, the law, for the first time, addresses the paperwork burden in special education, putting in place several measures that streamline IEPs and other paperwork requirements. Other changes from previous legislation include raising the age at which transition plans are required, instituting measures that will make it easier for schools to discipline students with disabilities, and moving special education research to the

Institute of Education Sciences (IES). The new IDEA requires schools to implement measures to reduce the overrepresentation of students from diverse backgrounds in special education through means such as the following:

- Schools must document the degree to which the student's limited English proficiency contributes to learning and behavior problems, and special education is excluded if this is the most significant factor in the presenting problem.
- Schools may use methods other than the IQ-achievement discrepancy model to determine whether or not students have a learning disability.
- Districts with significant overidentification of minority students must implement pre-referral programs to reduce the number of students inappropriately referred to special education.
- To reduce overidentification and misidentification of students from diverse backgrounds for special education, funding is provided to train school personnel in effective teaching strategies and positive behavior interventions and supports.
- Assessments must be provided and administered in the language and form most likely to yield accurate information on what the child knows and can do academically, developmentally, and functionally.

Unfortunately, the new IDEA's financial provisions offer little relief for the cost of special education. Rather than mandating full funding for special education, the new IDEA maintained the current funding system, providing a "glide path" by which the federal government would pay 40% of the excess cost of educating students with disabilities by 2010. Nevertheless, overall IDEA has more positives than negatives for children with disabilities and special educators.

## ENCULTURATION AND THE CLD STUDENT

Each CLD student has arenas in which he or she will attempt to conform to the culture of the classroom and school and other arenas in which he or she will resist the system. An awareness of these cultural productions will allow teachers not to make assumptions about a student's academic needs, desires, or preferences based on cultural overgeneralizations. Rather, the teacher will attempt to get know to each student as an individual, to understand why the student accepts or rejects certain aspects of the school's culture, and perhaps even to work with the student to transform those aspects of the social and academic setting that he or she opposes.

The Nature-Nurture Triangle in Figure 9 illustrates a model for working with CLD learners, which aids in understanding and being able to distinguish difference from disability. The bottom, or *Basics*, tier represents all the things we share as human beings. This is the place where differences and disabilities become most fundamentally apparent: variations in height, color, and gender are differences, while variations in sensory, linguistic, and cognitive processing

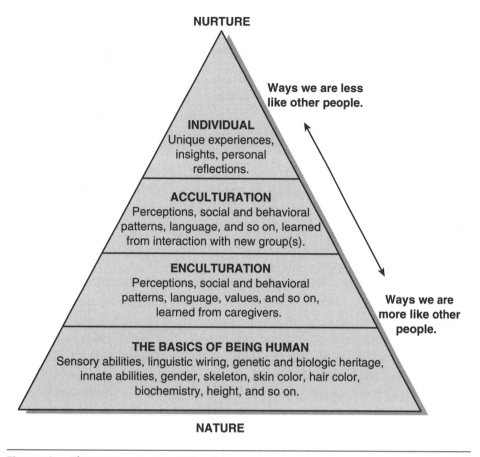

**Figure 9**   The Nature-Nurture Triangle

abilities could be considered disabilities in some cultures. Approximately 10% of all human populations have some type of condition considered disabling by the community into which they are born (Baca & Cervantes, 2003). These disabilities can be of prenatal, perinatal, or postnatal origin. They can include various organic exceptionalities, such as varying degrees of impairment of hearing and sight, skeletal and musculature abnormalities, hormonal deficiencies, neurological dysfunctions, and other physical, sensory, anatomical, or mental characteristics considered disabling by the birth community. The next tier, *Enculturation,* is where one learns how to interpret the world—a process that begins at birth and includes beliefs, humor, language, and behavior expectations, among other characteristics. The third tier is *Acculturation,* which in this model refers to adaptation to a new culture, language, interaction, or environment. The final tier of the triangle represents all the rest of our *Individual* differences that arise from our experiences, education, associations, and so on.

## Enculturation

Of the four tiers in the Nature-Nurture triangle, Enculturation is the most relevant to culturally and linguistically diverse students in US and Canadian schools. Enculturation is the process by which a person acquires his or her native culture. The diversity of cultures that this process brings to our classrooms makes mainstream standardized education challenging because language and culture issues compound the range of diverse abilities we accommodate within our schools.

Enculturation starts with the newborn child's first interactions with the world, beginning with significant people such as parents, siblings, midwives, or doctors. The presence of particular sounds, sights, smells, and other environmental stimuli are also part of this process. All human beings grow up within a cultural context, and enculturation teaches children how to respond to, interpret, and perceive the culture within which they are reared. "Culture consists of whatever it is one has to know or believe in order to operate in a manner acceptable to its members" (Goodenough, 1957, p. 167). Culture is how we organize our behaviors, communication, values, and emotions; it is the patterns of interaction, communication, socialization, and education held in common by a particular group of people.

All cultural groups teach their children; however, *how* and *what* is taught (and *why*) varies considerably among cultures. This education is generally not a formal process; rather, it is a consequence of child rearing practices handed down from generation to generation. As a result of different child rearing practices, which in turn are based upon different beliefs about how things are to be done, children develop varying ways of dealing with adults and peers and of interacting with the world in general. An example of such differences is the diversity of opinions about dependence and independence. In some cultures, caregivers encourage passiveness and contentedness in children. This is based upon a belief that the toddler or child is independent and must be taught to be dependent. Caregivers and teachers spend a lot of energy during formative years in these communities working on group skills such as sharing and working for the good of the group. Sometimes this is done by carrying the child around close to the caregiver, having the child sleep with family members, having children start caring for their siblings at an early age, and responding immediately or preemptively when the child begins to display discomfort. In other cultures, caregivers encourage assertiveness and self-direction, and adults spend a lot of energy teaching the child or toddler how to function independently. Examples of this are having the child sleep alone, letting the child continue crying without responding, and telling a male child that he must be "a little man."

Another area of diverse enculturation is how people regard intentional actions and one's control over these actions. In some cultures, toddlers are considered to have intentionality in their actions and are expected to think and act as a social partner in interactions. These children are expected to understand that they are responsible for their actions and in control of their interactions (internal locus of control). In other cultures, toddlers are not considered to have intentionality and are not expected to think or act as a social partner (external locus of control). Both of these have implications for educators in US American public schools, where our culture expects internal locus of control and full individual responsibility for actions, even when the individual is still very young.

A third difference in enculturation that impacts education is perceptions of the status of children. On the one hand, there are families and communities in which the child is not encouraged to talk to those older or higher in rank. Caregivers and teachers will instruct the child not to speak to elders or people of higher ranking except under specific interaction rules. On the other hand, there are families and communities in which the child is expected to speak to everyone. Caregivers and teachers will encourage the child to talk to anyone and will consider there to be something wrong with the child if he or she does not do so.

## Four Components of Culture

As mentioned previously, culture is not a material phenomenon but rather an organization of factors including behaviors, values, and emotions. It shapes the way we think (*cognition*), the way we interact (*behavior*), the way we communicate (*language*), and the way we transmit knowledge to the next generation (*education*). These components of culture are not static; they change continually from the influence of both internal and external circumstances. Where several cultures are in contact, or where there is much movement and communication between social groups and geographic areas, some overlapping and blurring of cultural boundaries will occur. In addition, cultural identity and cognitive development occur concurrently and are enmeshed with one another. Both describe perceptions and the manner in which we develop awareness of and interpret our environment. Any effort to assess or provide intervention with cognitive development must be done within the cultural context. Edward T. Hall (1983) likened this cognitive cultural base to the hardwiring of a computer—the essential difference between an IBM and a Mac. One cannot become the other; this does not mean, however, that they cannot communicate or work effectively together. This is where the "software" or learned behaviors come in; that is, once our basic operating system is in place, we can learn new languages, gestures, and customs while still retaining our fundamental processes.

Cognition, the first component of culture, is the process of perceiving, attending, thinking, remembering, and knowing (Blumenthal, 1977). This process begins before birth and continues throughout life. One product of cognitive development is a person's cognitive learning style, which is the stable, typical, and consistent way in which individuals select and organize environmental data. Another outcome of cognitive development is the formation of one's preferred learning style. In essence, a preferred learning style is the specific style or strategy that each student uses to respond to the instructional environment and to accomplish the instructional task at hand. This is not a constant pattern of behavior; a person's preferred learning style changes with age and experience—especially with exposure to novel cognitive and learning strategies. Cognitive development and cognitive and preferred learning styles depend largely on a student's cultural background and experience because they are directly shaped and influenced by it. Identifying these styles becomes an instructionally meaningful part of the assessment of CLD students because it contributes directly to the development of appropriate interventions, problem solving, and IEPs.

To exemplify another product of this cognitive cultural base, consider the fact that all human beings can physiologically perceive the spectrum of angstroms that we interpret as colors (unless having specific impairments). Each cultural/linguistic community divides the spectrum into colors differently. We see the same colors but do not organize them or have the same model of them in our minds or in our cognitive structures. For example, in English we say the spectrum is made up of red, orange, yellow, green, blue, and purple or violet. We even have names for the colors beyond red (infrared) and violet (ultraviolet) that are not normally perceptible. Other Indo-European languages organize these colors in the same way, using different but related terms. In Spanish, they are *rojo, anaranjado, amarillo, verde, azul,* and *morado,* in some dialects. In French, they are *rouge, orange, jaune, vert, bleu,* and *pourpre.* And in Latin, *ruber, luteus, flavus, viridius, caeruleus,* and *viola.* However, in Navajo, an Athabascan language, there are only three basic colors in the traditional spectrum: *li'chii* (reds to oranges), *li'tso* (yellow), and *dootl'izh* (greens, blues, and bluish greens). In Yup'ik, an Inuit language, the colors are red, yellow, green, and blue. This is not a physiological difference but, rather, a cognitive difference reflecting distinct ways of classifying colors and thereby of organizing the environment. A traditional Navajo or Yup'ik child can certainly learn the English or Spanish words for the colors, and linguists have invented new terms in Navajo and Yup'ik to fill in "the gaps." It is necessary that U.S. American teachers keep in mind that even though students from linguistic backgrounds other than English are physically able to see the same color spectrum that English speaking children are, they may not be accustomed to the division of colors present in English. Such students may present difficulties in the classroom when asked to differentiate between colors that, for them, fall into the same category (e.g., requesting a Navajo child to select the "blue" crayon, while his or her cognitive organization places all colors between blue and green under the category of "dootl'izh").

The second cultural component is behavior, which can be reflected in a student's conduct and interactions at school. For example, some cultures value individual contributions to the success of the group more than the success of the individual. Many Native American and Asian cultures will shun or ridicule an individual who appears to act apart from the group. Since much of the assessment conducted to identify learning and behavior problems isolates and singles out the individual student, assessment may in fact compound the student's problems in the classroom and in the home. The fear of being seen as different by peers may affect the student's performance during individually administered assessment procedures. During group assessment, the CLD student may want to assist other students and may not pay attention to personal performance. In addition, students from cultures that value indirectness and distance as evidence of appropriate behavior may not respond positively to the use of touching or praise as reinforcement strategies. These students' interpretations of "time out" and other teaching and behavior management techniques common in the United States may be quite different from the teacher's intent when utilizing those techniques. Inappropriate responses may lead the teacher to suspect the presence of a disabling condition.

Differences in experiential background also affect CLD students' responses to various elements of the curricula in U.S. American schools. The use of inquiry techniques, behavior contracting, active processing, and other individualized instructional strategies is very dependent on prior experience. Role expectations and the ability to make quick cause-and-effect associations are prerequisite skills for the optimal effectiveness of many strategies. If a diverse student lacks the appropriate response to the instructional strategies commonly used in the United States, this compounds their learning and behavior problems. Teachers frequently mistake this lack of appropriate response for the presence of a disabling condition.

Some of the diverse students' responses to the school environment may be due to previous school experiences, in addition to cultural differences. Students who have been in school systems in other countries generally know basic school procedures, such as raising their hands for attention, asking permission to do something, and recess and lunchroom behaviors. However, they may be unfamiliar with particular instructional strategies, such as independent or silent reading rather than group recitation, or discovery learning rather than rote memorization. Their inappropriate responses to silent reading, discovery learning, or other activities may be disruptive or troublesome to the teacher and can result in a referral.

Diverse students with no school experience may be unfamiliar with particular instructional strategies, as well as with the basic operational expectations of the school and classroom. They may not know how or when to ask for assistance or permission, may not be familiar with appropriate school behavior in or out of the classroom, and may not have had any exposure to academic language. These students will need to acculturate not only to U.S. American culture but also to the culture of school itself. Many "newcomers" programs provide this type of assistance.

The third cultural component, language, can be evidenced not only in differences in the actual words used, but also in discourse patterns. In relation to students' needs, in English the expectation is that we name the specific thing we are concerned about (for example, a child's learning behavior) and then "stick to the point" and "not beat around the bush." The expectation in Spanish is that our point will include its impact within the family context. In Slovak (and other Slavic languages), it is expected that one will keep the cultural history in mind or use it to reference the matter under discussion. In Japanese, with its context-embedded discourse structures, a speaker is expected to convey the point of concern without direct reference to it (Kaplan, 1966). In Navajo (and many other Native American languages), if a speaker does not include all aspects of the child in the discussion, he or she is seen as incomplete, inconsiderate, or as not having the child's best interests in mind.

Since culture has such a comprehensive effect upon the thinking, perceptions, and interaction patterns of individuals, practitioners must be familiar with the cultural and sociolinguistic background of their students, particularly of those students with learning and behavior problems. Culturally-based assumptions about what students should learn, how and where they should learn it, as well as why and when they will need this knowledge are the foundations of our educational system. Students reared in a different cultural environment will have learned a different body of knowledge and will have learned it in different ways. Education professionals must be sensitive to the cultural and sociolinguistic backgrounds of CLD students and must consider how these differences may affect a student's performance during the instructional process.

To conclude, in addition to identifying the range of academic and behavior performance for students with learning and behavior problems, school personnel must also consider sociocultural factors of diverse learners in their evaluation. The key sociocultural factors to be identified during the assessment of diverse students include: (1) cultural and linguistic background, (2) patterns of sociolinguistic development, (3) experiential background, (4) cognitive learning styles, and (5) stage and pattern of acculturation. Information about these sociocultural factors is available through a comprehensive review of existing student records, interviews, and observations, and by testing, work sampling, and analytic teaching. School personnel need to analyze differences in response to the school environment to determine if they are really examples of cultural diversity. When the student's inappropriate behavior in the school is clearly not due to cultural differences or to lack of school experience, the teacher may proceed with the analysis of other possible causes, including the presence of a disabling condition. Experiential differences affect both classroom behavior and performance on assessment devices. Practitioners who work with diverse students need to be aware of and be able to identify experiential differences in order to improve the assessment and instruction of diverse students.

# JOSÉ CASE STUDY

Throughout this book, an actual student, José, will be used as a case study to illustrate the four tiers of the PRISIM process and some of the additional issues to be considered when separating difference from disability. The case study will include evaluations, test results, observations, and interviews.

## PRISIM 1 José's Profile at Enrollment

José was eight when his family immigrated to the United States from Peru. His father and uncle are employed in seasonal farm labor in their new community. His aunt and mother work in a meatpacking plant. José's grandmother helps take care of him and his seven siblings and cousins. She is considered a healer in their native community. She speaks only Quechua, an indigenous language from the Andes Mountains, which is the family's native language. José, his cousins, and his older siblings attended school in Peru and speak Spanish fairly fluently. Both of his parents speak Spanish, though with limited fluency. The family is involved in the local Catholic Church, which has a large immigrant and migrant membership. There are some Mexican food stores and restaurants in the community.

## PRISIM 1 Learning Foundation Issues

Culturally, he is from a traditional indigenous group that resides on both the western and eastern sides of the Andes in South America. His family is intact and extended, giving him substantial support for cognitive and linguistic development. Linguistically, his Quechua is developmentally appropriate, but as he never received schooling in his home language, he has very limited cognitive academic schema in Quechua. After two years of school in Peru, first and second grades, he has an appropriate developmental level of Spanish (i.e., at the Speech Emergent, beginning bilingual level). Environmentally, he has access to safety, food, clothing, and shelter, and he has supportive, responsive relationships at home. His family worked hard in Peru to make sure José was able to attend the nearest village school. Educationally, he has two years of elementary schooling, albeit in Spanish—a language other than his home language or English.

As stated at the beginning of this chapter, the goal for the receiving school district is to promote and sustain the following:

- José's access to safety, food, clothing, and shelter
- Quality preparation of effective education professionals and support staff who will be working with José
- The adequacy of school facilities and resources available to José and his family
- Consistent use of culturally and linguistically responsive, evidence-based practices when working with José
- Supportive, responsive relationships between José and school personnel

Familiarity with José's experience, culture, and language background will be very important when planning initial instruction. Receiving school personnel should begin research for making decisions about service placement by identifying language background, language proficiency, level of acculturation, prior schooling, and other instructionally meaningful data.

# Establishing and Supporting Resiliency 2

**PRISIM Step 2. Establishing and Supporting Resiliency**

*Gathering information about CLD students' educational resiliency (i.e., what skills and strengths the diverse students bring with them that will facilitate achieving to the best of their ability). Providing differentiated learning support to all learners that promotes and sustains resiliency in a developmentally appropriate manner. Monitoring the effectiveness of these strategies and instructions by a problem solving with progress monitoring approach (e.g., RTI or RTII). In programs using the tiered RTI or RTII model, this step coincides with Tier I.*

Resiliency-based models for providing instructional and support services help all children achieve to the best of their abilities by reducing risk factors and enhancing the strengths and inherent resiliency of learners. These models are also sometimes referred to as *prevention models*. The PRISIM pyramid approach described in the Introduction to this book is an expansion on the resiliency-based model.

Wolpow, Johnson, Hertel, and Kincaid (2009) define resiliency as the ability of an individual family, or community, to withstand and rebound from adversity. Resiliency research is the study of how some students, despite stressors in their lives, manage to adapt and in some cases thrive. Resiliencies are assets that can be both external (things that other people provide for children or youth) and internal (things that develop

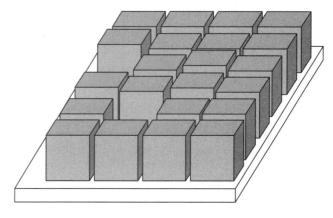

**Figure 10**   Building a Layer of Strategies to Support Resiliency

within the learners or children themselves). According to Berliner and Benard (1995), there are four categories of external assets and four categories of internal assets that are common to healthy, productive, and competent children who have past experiences of severe adversity. Many of the studies on resiliency were drawn from children who lived in the most severe of conditions, including children from concentration camps; children from abusive, criminal or substance-abusing homes; and children living in poverty or affected by gang participation. Normally, these children would be labeled as "at-risk" and would be provided programs designed to eliminate or mitigate those conditions. However, one consistent finding emerged from this research: Nearly two-thirds of the children studied did *not* develop high-risk behaviors. What was unique about those individuals? Are there personal traits and environmental characteristics that foster those traits in resilient children throughout their schooling years and into their adult lives? Berliner and Benard (1995) identified the personal traits common to children who had overcome severe risks in their lives.

1. **Social competence:** The ability to establish and sustain positive, caring relationships; to maintain a sense of humor; and to communicate compassion and empathy.

2. **Resourcefulness:** The ability to critically, creatively, and reflectively make decisions; to seek help from others; and to recognize alternative ways to solve problems and resolve conflicts.

3. **Autonomy:** The ability to act independently and exert some control over others engaged in risky or dysfunctional behaviors.

4. **Sense of purpose:** The ability to foresee a bright future for oneself, to be optimistic, and to aspire to educational and personal achievement.

Berliner and Benard (1995) concluded that the traits that "make up an individual's resilient nature are fostered or reinforced by caring relationships that are trusting, compassionate and respectful; high expectations that are explicitly communicated and adequately supported; and meaningful opportunities for engaging in valued family, school and civic activities" (pp. 3–4). Long-term studies have been conducted in many diverse communities with children of parents with mental challenges, children of teenaged parents, children raised in extreme poverty, as well as with orphaned and refugee progeny who survived the trauma of wars and famine. The majority of these studies revealed that resiliency is primarily a process. Though some individuals have genetic tendencies, such as a cheerful temperament, that may contribute to their resiliency, most of the characteristics associated with resiliency can be learned and supported. All of this research confirms that the more we communicate our genuine concern for the safety, well-being, and academic and personal success of our students, the more likely we are to succeed in meeting their needs. This is true for all students, regardless of background or the severity of past social or personal conditions.

Since 2000, the Center for Research on Education, Diversity, and Excellence (CREDE) has been working to find out which features make the difference for at-risk ELLs from Latino backgrounds. Approximately 1,000 fourth and fifth graders in three elementary schools participated in the CREDE study (Padrón, Waxman, Brown, & Powers, 2000). All three of the schools had a majority of students considered at risk of school failure, with more than 80% from high-poverty, language minority families. The students selected for systematic observation and interviews were identified by their teachers as either resilient (motivated, high achievers with good attendance) or nonresilient (the opposite of resilient). Some of the differences found between the two sets of students included the following: (1) resilient students had a more positive perception of their teachers, their classroom environment, and their own reading ability; (2) resilient students were more likely to speak their home language (Spanish) outside of the classroom; and (3) resilient students tended to use stronger learning strategies for reading, such as telling a story in their own words or outlining the main points. The study results suggested that a student's educational resiliency can be upgraded by instructional strategies that help foster close relationships, build social and academic competencies, value diversity, and provide other necessary support. In most of the classrooms observed, however, teachers relied on whole class systematic drills designed to help students prepare for state-mandated tests rather than encouraging cooperative, multicultural learning.

Findings from the study have been used to develop PIRP, the Pedagogy to Improve Resiliency Program. PIRP was successfully piloted in a Texas elementary school with a predominately lower-socioeconomic, Latino population (Waxman & Padrón, 2002). The way in which these resiliency strengths can be facilitated and enhanced is based on two direct instruction steps: Step 1: Identify and build instruction upon sociocultural resiliency; Step 2: Identify and individualize for diverse cognitive learning strategies. These steps must be implemented in a manner that is inclusive and not exclusive, developmental and not remedial, comprehensive, and resiliency-based.

Another example of a resiliency-based instructional model designed for culturally and linguistically diverse children is the Neekon project that was facilitated by the University of Oklahoma American Indian Center in 1995. During Neekon, Kickapoo Indian children attending a Head Start program in the Kickapoo Nation received specific instruction in developing coping skills, enhancing self-concept and self-esteem, and developing communication strategies for speaking to caring adults about abusive or dangerous situations in their lives. Head Start staff received training in identifying risk behaviors in three- to four-year-old children and in providing direct intervention when needed. Families participating in Neekon received assistance with accessing tribal and community support services and were guided to programs to help with substance abuse and other mental health issues.

The following are findings from research on fostering resiliency cited by Wolpow et al. (2009):

1. Foster resiliency and hope; provide unconditional positive regard in a safe and caring environment.

2. Always empower, never disempower. In other words, be assertive in addressing inappropriate student conduct; however, avoid any controlling method that might resemble the behaviors of perpetrators of violence.

3. Set up situations for students who have built some resiliency to help themselves by helping others.

4. Maintain high expectations, reasonable limits, and consistent routines. Limits are most appropriate when they are immediate, related, age-appropriate, proportional, and delivered in a calm and respectful voice.

5. Increase connections with any pro-social person.

6. Focus on both the effective and the affective, requiring instructors to embed instruction with compassionate qualities of the heart, such as courage, commitment, belief, and intuitive understanding.

One tool for identifying, measuring, and monitoring resiliencies in diverse learners is the Resiliency Checklist. An example of the tool is available in Figure 12, in the case study at the end of this section. On the Resiliency Checklist, if more than 40% of the items in any of the resiliency areas are checked off, it indicates that the student has substantial strength in that area. These strengths can be supported and used to facilitate further growth and achievement. The following is a list of areas in which students may have high resiliency and characteristics of academic programs from which those students would most benefit:

- Students with high resiliency in *acculturation* will benefit from programs that facilitate and honor their ability to walk in both cultures and to use both modes of communication.
- Students with high resiliency in *cognitive learning styles* will benefit from classroom strategies that build upon their strengths and teachers who modify their teaching styles to accommodate diverse cognitive learning styles within their classrooms.
- Students with high resiliency in *culture and language* would most benefit from programs that value and honor students' culture and language and that use instructional strategies that facilitate sharing this knowledge and transferring and integrating skills from the home language and culture to the new language and culture.
- Students with high resiliency in *experiential background* will benefit from techniques and strategies that build on their prior experiences and facilitate making connections and associations between the known and the unknown.
- Students with high resiliency in *sociolinguistic development* will benefit from approaches that focus on language transfer and the relationship between communication forms from the first and second language.

If less than 40% of the items in any of the five areas are checked off, it indicates that the student needs intervention and assistance in this area. This allows the educator or team to target a specific area for early intervention and intensive monitoring and guides them in making better instructional decisions for this student. Some students may have several areas that need attention. In these cases, the teacher or team will need to prioritize the student's intervention needs, rank ordering the five sociocultural resilience areas from highest percentile to lowest.

# COGNITION AND LANGUAGE

Lev Vygotsky (1896–1934), a Russian psychologist, believed that thought and language develop through communication with other people. He espoused a theory of cognitive development known as Sociocultural Theory, with the position that human activities take place in a cultural setting and cannot be understood apart from these settings (Vygotsky, 1962). He did not view social interaction merely as an influence on a child's cognitive development, but rather as the origin of higher mental processes, such as problem solving. His writings emphasize the roles of historical, cultural, and social factors in cognition and argue that language is the most important symbolic tool provided by society. Vygotsky (1978) stated:

> Every function in the child's cultural development appears twice: First, on the social level, and later, on the individual level; First, between people (interpsychological) and then inside the child (intrapsychological). This applies equally to voluntary attention, to logical memory, and to the formation of concepts. All the higher functions originate as actual relationships between individuals. (p. 57)

Vygotsky's (1962) theory involves the idea that the potential for cognitive development depends on the "zone of proximal development" (ZPD), a level of development attained when children engage in social or language interaction within their range of competence. The range of skill that can be developed with adult guidance or peer collaboration exceeds what can be attained alone.

Vygotsky's Sociocultural Theory was an attempt to explain consciousness as the end product of socialization. For example, in the learning of language, our first utterances with peers or adults are for the purpose of communication, but once mastered, they become internalized and allow for inner speech. Vygotsky's theory may be summarized as having two principles: (1) cognitive development is limited to a certain range at any given age, and (2) full cognitive development requires social interaction. Cutting off this important developmental process in speakers of languages other than English is counterproductive for long-term cognitive and academic development. Because of this, the author strongly recommends that teachers facilitate the use and retention of students' primary, home, or heritage languages within the academic setting. This can be done within any classroom, even those without a bilingual teacher, through the use of constructive structured language activities (e.g., students discussing the content of a lesson with one another in their home languages). The students can then move on to sharing their thoughts with the teacher about the lessons.

There are numerous scholars who support Vygotsky's theories. Cummins (1981, 1989) advocated instruction that consists of genuine dialogue between the student and teacher, as well as student-to-student collaborative talk. In addition, the importance of using the home language or dialect within structured classroom activities has been documented by research to provide the following benefits: building positive self-esteem, providing a foundation for learning, supporting survival skills, strengthening identification, strengthening resiliency, supporting family ties, and strengthening self-concept (Thomas & Collier, 1997, 2002; Wong Fillmore, 1991).

## A BRIEF REVIEW OF LANGUAGE ACQUISITION ISSUES

A foreign language is both acquired and learned. According to Krashen (1981), acquisition amounts to a functional mastery of some aspect of a language, such as a word or grammar structure, that does not have to be translated from the first language because you "just know it." On the other hand, learning is a conscious process whereby information about a language is stored in the mind, and one accesses and uses it consciously to translate to or from the target language. To some extent, acquisition is subconscious or covert, and learning is conscious or overt. Language learners in typical settings perform both acquisition and learning simultaneously.

As noted by de Valenzuela (2000), the complexity of the language learning/ acquisition process is further increased by the fact that language can be seen as a combination of components, rather than as a single matter. As described previously, we can discuss the social and cultural components of language. In addition, when we think about language development in schools, we think about the *form* of language. We can also talk about the *content* of language and about language *use.* Children are socialized to use language in ways that are deemed appropriate in their culture and home community. The language that a child has been socialized to use may be very different from the language used in the school environment. As discussed previously, within different cultural groups there are different expectations for how, when, and where children speak to adults. Direct questioning of adults by children may be permitted, indeed encouraged, in some communities, and strongly discouraged in others. These differences extend to nonverbal communication, such as eye contact, as well. Without understanding how culturally and linguistically diverse children have been socialized to use language, educators who are not from their students' speech community may misidentify a language difference for a language disorder. Therefore, it is important to understand the culture and speech community of a child before assuming there is a disability (Minami & Ovando, 1995).

Terms such as *syntax, morphology,* and *phonology* are used about linguistic *form.* Syntax and morphology refer to the grammatical system of a language. Syntax governs the use of different word classes (such as nouns and verbs) and how these words are combined to form intelligible and grammatical sentences. Morphology refers to the rule system that governs how words are put together from smaller grammatical parts, such as root words, prefixes, and suffixes. There is an internalized rule system for putting together sounds as a phonological system. De Valenzuela (2000) gave the example of the manner in which the phonological system of English prohibits certain types of consonant clusters in the beginning of words, thus making it difficult for native English speakers to correctly pronounce the names of the following cities: Mbandake (Zaire); Mtwara (Tanzania); and Mpika, Mzimba, and Shiwa Ngandu (Zimbabwe). This is because the phonological system of English excludes such consonant clusters at the beginning of words. Phonological rules also govern whether the plural *s* sounds like an *s* (as in *cats*) or a *z* (as in *dogs*). No one consciously learns the rules of phonology, morphology, or syntax in their native language. In fact, most people would be hard pressed to explain why they form words and sentences in the way they do—most of our knowledge about our native language is acquired and thus unconscious.

We can also talk about the *content* of language. When we talk about word meanings, we are talking about semantics. *Semantics* refers to more than just vocabulary knowledge, or the meaning of words. Semantics also refers to the function of words. Understanding how words function is very important in child language research because oftentimes one word will assume many functions, depending on the context. For example, "daddy go," could mean a variety of different things. In one instance, it could mean "daddy isn't here." In another context, it could be a command from a child for daddy to go somewhere.

More recently, linguists have also started talking about language *use*, or *pragmatics* (de Valenzuela, 2000). This area is concerned with the multitude of ways that people can say things and how this varies in different situations. Pragmatics involves language form and content, as well as other facets of language such as intonation, hesitancies, pauses, loudness, and rate. Speakers should be able to switch styles of speech according to different communicative contexts. For example, the way students address their peers is most likely very different from how they would greet the school principal. Pragmatic language skills are learned as well as acquired, along with knowledge and use of syntax, morphology, phonology, and semantics. Children learn very quickly the language use rules of their community and dialect, although, as with any linguistic ability, full competence takes years to develop. It is essential to remember that pragmatics, like other aspects of language, varies from one language to another. For example, ELL students may bring assumptions about certain aspects of language use from their first language, such as loudness, intonation, or turn taking, that may not be the same in English.

## Language Variation

Is the English spoken by university professors and news anchors on nationally televised broadcasts inherently better than that spoken by blue-collar workers in the Appalachian Mountains? Socially, Standard American English, or that spoken by most professors and broadcasters, is more prestigious than Appalachian English. But is Standard American English really "better" or more "correct" than other dialects of English? According to the linguistic universals, all are equally functional language varieties. In addition, these universals support that no dialect, regardless of prestige, is more or less complex than any other. From a purely linguistic perspective, all languages and dialects are able to convey equally complex information and are equally able to adapt to new situations, such as developing vocabulary for new technologies. Speaking on a functional level, the question of better depends on the social situation. Clearly, there are different standards for language use in different contexts: Using Standard American English at an informal family gathering when that family speaks a different dialect of English may come across as arrogant and stilted. The appropriateness of a particular language variety is determined by a speaker's ability to effectively convey a message, including the relevant social information, within specific contexts, and the mark of a truly accomplished communicator is the ability to vary speaking styles according to the social situation. Therefore, although acquiring Standard English (or Standard Spanish, for that matter) may be an appropriate academic goal, it is imperative that teachers understand that students' native language varieties are as valid, functional, appropriate, and grammatical as the standard dialect. Nonprestigious forms should never be considered broken or corrupt—they are legitimate and appropriate forms of speech in the students' home community and educators must demonstrate respect for their students' native language(s) or dialect(s).

Often, there are quite a few misconceptions about dialect. For example, the distinction between what is considered a language and what is considered a dialect may not be as clear as many think (Trudgill, 2000). Lippi-Green (1997) stated that linguists typically use the term *dialect* to "talk about language differences over geographic space . . . . [However,] laypersons often associate the word dialect as something less developed, capable, or worthy, and hence, always subordinate to a language" (pp. 247–248). Actually, whether a linguistic variety is considered a dialect or a language often has more to do with the political context than the amount of difference between two varieties. For example, Cantonese and Mandarin are considered dialects of Chinese. However, they are so different from each other that speakers of these dialects require translators to understand each other. In contrast, there is a high degree of mutual intelligibility between several Scandinavian languages. This should remind us that we need to be very careful when using interpreters and translators or evaluating the validity of standardized test results—if the language variety spoken by the student differs significantly from that of the interpreter or test, then there is a real possibility for miscommunication and inaccurate test results.

Another related idea that educators must remember is that each country or region is likely to have a national or regional dialect that is considered to be the standard or prestigious variety. This can differ greatly from the dialect that is considered the prestigious variety of that language within the United States. It is as inappropriate to assume that a student from Mexico should speak Castilian Spanish or that a student from El Salvador should speak the prestigious dialect of Mexico as it is to demand that US American students learn to speak standard British English. Educators must become informed about the rich linguistic knowledge that culturally and linguistically diverse students and their families bring with them, rather than comparing them against often inappropriate linguistic standards.

### Basic Interpersonal Communication Skills Versus Cognitive Academic Language Proficiency

It is not unusual to have students who are non-English speakers with proficiency in another language referred for assessment because of language disabilities. Rueda and Mercer (1985) observed that speech therapists were regularly involved with limited English speaking students, while specialists in language difference (i.e., bilingual/ESL educators) were almost never involved. The identification of ELL and LEP students as language-disabled when they exhibit auditory perception and expressive problems in English conflicts with the provisions of US federal law and other legislation and litigation. Such students can be said to have a language disability only if they demonstrate receptive and expressive language problems in both their native language and in English.

Sometimes teachers refer diverse students with learning and behavior problems because they think that limited English proficiency is not an issue; that is, they observe the student using English on a regular basis and conclude that language transition is no longer a factor. However, they may be confusing basic interpersonal communication skills (BICS) for cognitive academic language proficiency (CALP). The acronyms BICS and CALP are part of a theory of language proficiency developed by Jim Cummins (1984) that reflects the differences between social and academic language. BICS, often referred to as *playground English* or *survival English*, is the basic language ability required for face-to-face communication where linguistic interactions are embedded in a situational context. This social language is context-embedded, meaning that it is often accompanied by gestures, visual clues, and expressions. This makes it relatively undemanding cognitively because it relies on the context to aid understanding. The length of time required to achieve age-appropriate levels of BICS, or social language, is one to two years. CALP, on the other hand, is the language ability required for academic achievement in a context-reduced environment. Examples of context-reduced environments include classroom lectures and textbook reading assignments. With minimal assistance, the length of time required to achieve age-appropriate levels of CALP, or academic language, is five to seven years. Table 1 is a graphic representation summarizing what research shows us about the length of time it takes to acquire various proficiency levels of an additional language. Table 1, Language Acquisition Grid, illustrates the normal stages of English language acquisition for CLD ELL students within public schools receiving one hour of assistance in English transition each day. The terms across the rows are adapted from Krashen (1981) and describe the various levels of acquisition. The length of time indicated below those terms represents the average length of time it takes for a student who does not speak English to achieve the indicated level of acquisition. Descriptions of what the student is able to do with language in the classroom context are indicated in the column beneath the descriptive term and length of time.

**Table 1** Language Acquisition Grid

| Preproduction | Early Production | Speech Emergent | Intermediate Fluency | Advanced Intermediate Fluency | Advanced Fluency |
|---|---|---|---|---|---|
| 0–6 months | 6 months–1 year | 1–2 years | 2–3 years | 3–5 years | 5–7 years |
| - Depends on context<br>- Has minimal receptive vocabulary<br>- Comprehends key words only<br>- Points, draws, or gestures responses<br>- May not produce speech<br>- Adjusting to US culture<br>- 0–500 receptive word vocabulary<br>- Able to observe, locate, label, match, show, classify, sort<br>- Beginning L2 (second language) sound symbol understanding<br>- Reads and writes if literate in L1 (first language) | - Speech is so halting and fragmentary as to make conversation virtually impossible<br>- Depends heavily on context<br>- Produces words in isolation<br>- Verbalizes key words<br>- Responds with one or two word answers or short phrases<br>- Points, draws, or gestures responses<br>- Mispronunciation<br>- Grammar errors<br>- 500–1,000 receptive word vocabulary<br>- Able to name, recall, draw, record, point out, underline, categorize, list<br>- Uses simple words, gestures, and drawings<br>- Beginning sound symbol understanding<br>- Reads and writes basic sight words in L2 if literate in L1 | - Pronunciation problems necessitate concentration on the part of the listener: occasionally may be misunderstood<br>- Short phrases<br>- Many mistakes in grammar<br>- Makes frequent errors of grammar and word order which occasionally obscure meaning<br>- Hears smaller elements of speech<br>- Functions on social level<br>- Uses limited vocabulary<br>- Between 1,000–6,000 receptive vocabulary<br>- Able to share, retell, follow, associate, organize, compare, restate, role-play<br>- Reads and writes basic sight words<br>- Reads and writes simple words/sentences in L2 if literate in L1 | - Simple sentences<br>- Produces whole sentences<br>- Makes some pronunciation and basic grammatical errors but is understood<br>- Responds orally and in written form<br>- Uses limited vocabulary<br>- Initiates conversation and questions<br>- Shows good comprehension<br>- Up to 7,000 receptive word vocabulary<br>- Able to tell, describe, restate, contrast, question, map, dramatize, demonstrate, give instructions<br>- Uses short sentences to inform and explain<br>- Reads and writes simple words/ sentences<br>- Reads and writes descriptive sentences in L2 if literate in L1 | - Can communicate thoughts<br>- Engages in and produces connected narrative<br>- Shows good comprehension<br>- Uses expanded vocabulary<br>- Makes complex grammatical errors<br>- Functions somewhat on an academic level<br>- Up to 12,000 receptive and active word vocabulary<br>- Able to imagine, create, appraise, contrast, predict, express, report, estimate, evaluate, explain, model<br>- Uses descriptive sentences and initiates conversations<br>- Reads and writes descriptive sentences<br>- Reads and writes complex sentences in L2 if literate in L1 | - Functions on academic level with peers<br>- Maintains two-way conversations<br>- Demonstrates decontextualized comprehension<br>- Uses enriched vocabulary<br>- Beyond 12,000 word vocabulary<br>- Able to relate, infer, hypothesize, outline, revise, suppose, verify, rewrite, justify, critique, summarize, illustrate, judge<br>- Native-like proficiency with social conversations<br>- Reads and writes complex sentences in L2 or in both languages if literate in L1 |

(adapted from Collier, 2008a)

With intensive assistance, educators can bring BICS down to one year and CALP down to approximately four years. BICS is much more easily and quickly acquired than CALP, but it is not sufficient to meet the cognitive and linguistic demands of an academic classroom (C. Baker & Jones, 1998; Cummins, 1984). This demonstrates why functional language screening is recommended for separating difference from disability.

## Cognitive Learning Style

As described in Step 1, cognition is the process of perceiving, thinking, remembering, and knowing. Formal education can affect the ability to develop and use cognitive processes. Many researchers agree that the differences in how we conceptually organize our environment result in characteristic ways of learning from our experiences. Examples of areas where the teacher and student may experience dissonance in cognitive style in the classroom include the following: style difference between student and teacher, emotional response to completing tasks, and understanding and applying cause and effect. The following examples are based on the seven cognitive styles in which the most common divergences exist between US American education professionals and their CLD learners. The categories have been compiled from research by Collier (2005), H. Gardner (1993), R. W. Gardner (1953), Palincsar (1986), and Palincsar and Brown (1987). A summary of this information is available in Table 2.

1. Style Divergence: Anxiety
    a. You respond differently to challenging tasks or responsibilities than your student.
    b. You and your student respond differently to changes in your classroom environment and setting.
    c. You and your student do not find challenges motivating to a similar degree.

2. Style Divergence: Categorization
    a. You and your student use different attributes to exclude or include similar items from a group.
    b. You and your student approach task or activity organization in a different sequence or order of implementation.
    c. You and your student do not separate items to similar levels of discrimination.

3. Style Divergence: Field
    a. Your student approaches task analysis from a different perspective and level than you or your expectations.
    b. You and your student create or perceive visual, kinesthetic, and auditory patterns differently from one another.
    c. Your student puts meaning together in ways that differ from your approach or intentions.

4. Style Divergence: Locus of Control

   a. Your student shows a different concept of accepting responsibility for actions than you expect or do yourself.

   b. You and your student differ in the kinds of circumstances you see as not your responsibility or as external to your control.

   c. You and your student differ in the degree of control you feel over what happens to you within the learning environment.

5. Style Divergence: Persistence

   a. Your student differs from you in the level and length of time required to concentrate upon a task or solve a problem.

   b. Your student uses or maintains a different level or degree of self-monitoring than you expect or do yourself.

   c. You and your student differ in your comfort with meeting deadlines and getting work done on time.

6. Style Divergence: Tolerance

   a. Your student shows a different level of comfort with fantasy than you expect or do yourself.

   b. You and your student have different approaches to the use of imagination in learning and teaching tasks.

   c. Your student shows a different response (level of comfort) to reality-based tasks, content, or learning than you expect or do yourself.

7. Style Divergence: Tempo

   a. You and your student differ in your level or degree of comfort with the pace of learning and teaching.

   b. Your student is more impulsive or cautious with answers, tasks, or problem solving than you expect or are yourself.

   c. Your student needs a different amount of time to consider the correctness of a response than you expect or do yourself.

**Table 2**  Diverse Cognitive Learning Styles

| |
|---|
| **1. Anxiety** |
| a) High: Tendency to perform less well when challenged by a difficult task |
| b) Low: Tendency to perform better when challenged by a difficult task |
| **2. Categorization** |
| a) Broad: Tendency to include many items in a category and lessen the risk of leaving something out |
| b) Narrow: Tendency to exclude doubtful items and lessen the probability of including something that does not belong |

**3. Field**

  a) Independent: Tendency to see everything as elements making up a whole: emphasis on the parts and not the whole

  b) Sensitive: Tendency to see the whole: difficulty separating the whole from its parts

**4. Locus of Control**

  a) Internal: Tendency to think of oneself as responsible for one's own behavior

  b) External: Tendency to see circumstances as beyond one's own control: luck or others are seen as responsible for one's behavior

**5. Persistence**

  a) High: Tendency to work until the task has been completed: seeks any necessary help

  b) Low: Tendency to short attention: inability to work on a task for very long

**6. Tolerance**

  a) High: Tendency to accept experiences that vary markedly from the ordinary or even from reality or the truth

  b) Low: Tendency to show a preference for conventional ideas and reality

**7. Tempo**

  a) Reflective: Tendency to take more time and generate more effort to provide appropriate responses

  b) Impulsive: Tendency to give first answer that comes to mind even if frequently wrong or inappropriate

As students successfully implement the primary strategies, secondary strategies may be introduced. By profiling each student with learning and behavior problems, the teacher obtains a comprehensive picture of his or her classroom relative to each cognitive learning style. This information is considered along with data obtained through student interviews and teacher observations of the student learning preferences. An additional benefit of student interviews (i.e., asking the students how, when, what, and where they learn best) is that students become more actively involved in and aware of their own learning processes. The open discussion of effective and ineffective cognitive learning strategies has been shown to be an important element in the retention, transferability, and utilization of strategies (Kurtz & Borkowski, 1984).

In conclusion, identifying the strengths of the student and implementing instruction based on these strengths is an effective way to build a resiliency-based instructional program. This establishes a foundation upon which academic achievement and the development of learning capacity can be built.

An evaluation of CLD students' resiliency strengths should encompass the following areas: acculturation, cognitive learning, culture and language, and experiential background. Teaching to a student's strengths can greatly improve his or her academic and social development; however, even when students are resilient and are receiving appropriate and relevant instruction for their developmental level, some students will still have specific learning and behavior problems that need to be addressed as quickly and as effectively as possible.

# JOSÉ CASE STUDY

Continuing the case study from the previous step (in Chapter 1), there are more than 20 Spanish-speaking students at Jose's new school, as well as a few Ukrainian, Hmong, Yup'ik, and Russian speakers. There is a certificated ESL teacher available within the district, and the school's staff members have some experience working with culturally and linguistically diverse students and families.

## Intervention at PRISIM 2 Tier 1

When José first enrolled in his new school district, his family was identified as limited English proficient and his father was given a Home Language Survey to complete and return to the school. The results of the Home Language Survey, José's evaluation at enrollment, and observations of José during his first weeks at the school were as follows:

1. José's country of origin is Peru.

2. The language José learned when first beginning to talk was Quechua.

3. The language José most frequently uses at home is Quechua, but he also uses some Spanish.

4. The language his parents most frequently speak to José is Quechua.

5. The language the primary caregiver (grandmother) speaks to José is Quechua.

6. The language most frequently spoken at home is Quechua.

7. José had academic instruction in a language other than English. He had two years of academic instruction in Spanish.

8. In describing the language understood by José, his father completed the form in the following manner:
   ❏ Understands only the home language and no English.
   ❏ Understand mostly the home language and some English (and Spanish).
   ❏ Understands the home language and English equally.

❏ Understands mostly English and some of the home language.

❏ Understands only English.

9. His father said he would prefer receiving communication from the school in Quechua, if possible.

## PRISIM 2 Tier 1: Language

Based on this Home Language Survey, José was given an oral Spanish proficiency test and two English proficiency tests, one an oral proficiency test and the other a state developed and required test to determine eligibility for ELL services. His score on the Spanish test showed that he was at the higher end of speech emergent and could communicate his basic classroom needs in Spanish. His score on the oral proficiency test in English was a 1, which meant that his English was at the preproduction level. His score on the state ELL services eligibility test was a 1 or *negligible English*. These test scores resulted in José being identified as eligible for ELL services. José received two hours of English instruction a day, as well as the assistance of a Spanish/English bilingual aide in his classroom during social studies and mathematics content lessons.

José quickly learned the morning greeting song and always picked up songs and rhymes very quickly. José appeared to like school, and his attendance was good. He was friendly and outgoing with his peers, and José always made an effort to be involved in whatever was going on in the classroom and on the playground. However, his limited English ability made it difficult for him to play with the children who did not speak Spanish. (See checklist excerpt in Figure 11.)

## PRISIM 2 Tier 1: Acculturation

An Acculturation Quick Screen (Collier, 2008b) was also completed on José, and he scored a 17 (see sample chart in Figure 12). This meant that he was *less acculturated*, and it was recommended that specific instructional strategies be employed. Students scoring as less acculturated do well with the assistance of a bilingual aide and the use of bilingual texts (Garcia, 2005; Kovelman, Baker, & Petitto, 2008). Another recommended strategy for less acculturated students is having the teacher use consistent sequences in all lessons (Mathes, Pollard-Durodola, Cárdenas-Hagan, Linan-Thompson, & Vaughn, 2007; Vaughn & Linan-Thompson, 2007). Content modification is another option for less acculturated ELL students (Brinton, Snow, & Wesche, 2003; Echevarria & Graves, 2006; McIntyre, Kyle, Chen-Ting, Kraemer, & Parr, 2009), as well as demonstrations and experience-based strategies (Echevarria, Vogt, & Short, 2004; Gibbons, 2002; Nessel & Dixon, 2008; Wasik, 2004). Providing cross-cultural counseling opportunities is also recommended for less acculturated ELL students (Burnham, Mantero, & Hooper, 2009; Landis, Bennett, & Bennett, 2004).

These are a cross section of strategies specific to less acculturated students that can be implemented in a Tier 1 setting. With the implementation of these strategies during his first year in school, José appeared to be adapting well to his new situation.

## PRISIM 2 Tier 1: Resiliency

A resiliency profile for José was developed using the Resiliency Checklist (Collier, 2008b). Figure 13 illustrates Jose's resiliency checklist. Here are the resiliency elements that were checked off as being present at the time José enrolled in the school:

1. There is quality verbal communication in the home in a language other than English.

2. There is behavioral guidance in the home consistent with a specific worldview.

3. The cultural values of the home support cooperative effort.

4. The family maintains communication with their linguistic and cultural community.

5. The family participates regularly in religious and social events within their community.

6. There is active support in the home for bilingual and bicultural development.

7. Adults in the home will provide encouragement and support for student's development.

8. Student makes an effort to increase attendance.

9. Adults in the family provide for the student's basic needs.

10. Early childhood development was appropriate to the culture and language.

11. Student displays curiosity and is ready to learn.

12. Student has prior classroom or formal education experience.

13. Student demonstrates a variety of survival strategies.

Based on this profile, classroom personnel used instructional strategies that maximized Jose's strengths and facilitated his adaptation to the curriculum and procedures used in the school. Some of these strategies implemented for José at Tier 1 were the same or similar to those for facilitating acculturation (e.g., the use of a bilingual aide and bilingual peers). In addition, other resiliency strengthening instructional strategies were provided, such as individualization and differentiation (Tomlinson, 1999), tapping into José's learning style differences (H. Gardner, 1993), and building his capacity to learn through listening (Fisher & Frey, 2004; Irvin & Rose, 1995).

| SOCIAL CLASSROOM | Quechua | Spanish | English |
|---|---|---|---|
| 1. Follows general directions (English with modeling) | ✓ | ✓ | ✓ |
| 2. Acts out common school activities | ✓ | ✓ | ✓ |
| 3. Points, draws, or gestures responses | ✓ | ✓ | ✓ |
| 4. Verbalizes key words (English when prompted) | ✓ | ✓ | ✓ |
| 5. Gives commands to peers | ✓ | ✓ | |
| 6. Exchanges common greetings | ✓ | ✓ | ✓ |
| 7. Uses limited vocabulary | ✓ | ✓ | |
| 8. Describes objects; describes people | ✓ | ✓ | |
| 9. Retells a familiar story | ✓ | ✓ | |
| 10. Initiates and responds to a conversation | ✓ | ✓ | |
| 11. Appears to attend to what is going on | ✓ | ✓ | ✓ |
| 12. Appropriately answers basic questions | ✓ | ✓ | |
| 13. Participates in sharing time | ✓ | ✓ | |
| 14. Narrates a simple story | ✓ | ✓ | |
| 15. Between 1000–6000 receptive vocabulary | ✓ | | |
| **Total social classroom interactions used in classroom** | 15 | 14 | 6 |
| **Total possible social classroom interactions** | **15** | **15** | **15** |

| ACADEMIC CLASSROOM | Spanish | English |
|---|---|---|
| 1. Follows specific directions for academic tasks | ✓ | |
| 2. Follows along during oral reading | ✓ | |
| 3. Understands teacher's discussion | ✓ | |
| 4. Uses sound/symbol association | ✓ | |
| 5. Decodes words | | |
| 6. Generates simple sentences | ✓ | |
| 7. Completes simple unfinished sentences | | |
| 8. Makes some pronunciation and basic grammatical errors but is understood | | |
| 9. Asks for clarification during academic tasks | | |
| 10. Asks and answers specific questions regarding topic | | |
| 11. Actively participates in class discussions; volunteers to answer questions | | |
| **Total academic language interactions used in classroom** | 5 | |
| **Total possible academic language interactions** | **40** | **40** |
| **Total classroom language interactions used in classroom** | 19 | 6 |
| **Total possible classroom language interactions** | **55** | **55** |

**Figure 11**  Excerpt From Initial Classroom Language Interaction Checklist (Collier, 2008a): Results for José

| Cultural/Environmental Factors | Information | Scores |
|---|---|---|
| 1. Number of years in United States/Canada | Three months | 1 |
| 2. Amount of time in school district | Three months | 1 |
| 3. Amount of time in ELL or bilingual program | None | 1 |
| 4. Native language proficiency | Quechua BICS | 3 |
| 5. English language proficiency | Does not speak English | 1 |
| 6. Bilingual proficiency | Quechua, some Spanish | 3 |
| 7. Ethnicity/Nation of origin | Quechua/Peru | 1 |
| 8. % in school speaking student's language/dialect | 1% Quechua | 6 |
| | **AQS Score Total** | 17 |

**Figure 12**   Excerpt From Initial Acculturation Quick Screen (Collier, 2010): Results for José

| ☑ | Selected Cross-Cultural Resiliency Factors |
|---|---|
| ✓ | Student attends events within the mainstream community. |
| ✓ | Student interacts with majority peers or majority cultural group. |
| | Student displays consistent sense of locus of control. |
| .5 | Student appears comfortable in cross-cultural interactions. |
| ✓ | The code switching in the student's speech shows an emerging understanding of English. |
| | Student appears comfortable switching linguistic/cultural environments. |
| 3.5 | Total out of 6    **% Checked: 59%** |
| | Student demonstrates consistent cognitive learning strategies. |
| | Student responds positively to variations in instructional strategies. |
| ✓ | Student responds positively to appropriate rewards/recognition. |
| ✓ | Student can apply cognitive learning strategies when given guided practice. |
| | Student can use self-monitoring strategies. |
| | Student can assist others in learning a task. |

*(Continued)*

**Figure 13** (Continued)

| | |
|---|---|
| 2 | Total out of 6 **% Checked: 33%** |
| ✓ | There is quality verbal communication in the home in a language other than English. |
| ✓ | There is behavioral guidance in the home consistent with a specific worldview. |
| ✓ | The cultural values of the home support cooperative effort. |
| .5 | The family maintains communication with their linguistic/cultural community. |
| ✓ | The family participates regularly in religious/social events within their community. |
| ✓ | There is active support in the home for bilingual and bicultural development. |
| 5.5 | Total out of 6 **% Checked: 92%** |
| ✓ | Adults in the home will provide encouragement and support for student's development. |
| ✓ | Student makes an effort to increase attendance. |
| ✓ | Adults in family provide for the student's basic needs. |
| | Family will provide support for student's learning (homework). |
| ✓ | Early childhood development was appropriate to culture/language. |
| ✓ | Student displays curiosity and is ready to learn. |
| ✓ | Student has prior classroom or formal education experience. |
| ✓ | Student has developmentally and linguistically appropriate literacy skills or pre-skills. |
| .5 | Student demonstrates variety of survival strategies. |
| 7.5 | Total out of 9 **% Checked: 83%** |
| ✓ | Student has good basic interpersonal communication skills in native language. |
| | Student has moderate to good cognitive academic language proficiency in native language. |
| .5 | BICS in English appears to be emerging. |
| | Student attempts to translate for others in the classroom. |
| | Student demonstrates emerging cognitive academic language proficiency in English. |
| ✓ | Student seeks assistance from peers. |
| | Code switching demonstrates emerging English syntax and vocabulary. |
| ✓ | Student can demonstrate content knowledge in his or her native language. |
| 3.5 | Total out of 8 **% Checked: 44%** |

**Figure 13**   Excerpt From Initial Resiliency Checklist (Collier, 2008a): Results for José

# Instructional Intervention and Differentiated Instruction 3

**PRISIM Step 3. Instructional Intervention and Differentiated Instruction**

*Screening to determine what diverse factors contribute significantly to emerging learning and behavior problems in order to identify learning and behavioral strategies that may effectively resolve these problems. Providing differentiated learning support and instruction to students who have specific learning and behavioral needs. In programs using the tiered RTI or RTII model, this step coincides with Tier 1 and Tier 2.*

The term *intervention* refers to the problem-solving process that ensues following an indication by a teacher or a concerned person that the student has some kind of learning or behavior problem (i.e., the student has been identified by the teacher, teacher assistance team, or another person at the building level but a formal referral for an evaluation has not occurred).

A key element of intervention is the implementation of curricular adaptations that attempt to resolve identified learning or behavior problems. Many schools now require some form of intervention prior to referral for formal assessment. An intervention period of six to eight weeks provides an opportunity to gather preliminary information and attempt initial interventions within the regular classroom setting. As mentioned

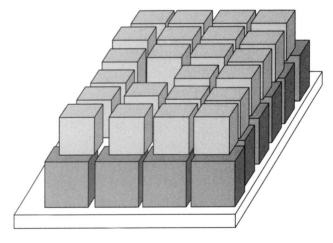

**Figure 14** Adding a Layer of Instructional Intervention Strategies to the PRISIM Pyramid

previously, culturally and linguistically diverse students may have learning or behavior problems due to acculturative stress or language and cultural differences rather than problems due to a possible disabling condition. However, a disabling condition that is masking or aggravating their learning and behavior adaptation to the mainstream curriculum may also be present. Thus, one purpose of interventions during the problem-solving process is to identify and address the sociocultural needs of the student. Research shows that intervention will satisfactorily address approximately 70% of the teacher's concerns about the diverse student (Baca & Cervantes, 2003). Unresolved learning and behavior problems after intensive intervention may require a referral to evaluation staff.

A successful intervention always involves the teacher, who gathers information about the student's background, culture and language, acculturation level, sociolinguistic development, and response to the school and classroom environment. If current language proficiency information is available and indicates that the student has limited English proficiency, the teacher modifies use of various assessment and intervention techniques to accommodate the student's language and cultural background. He or she may do this in collaboration with other professionals or with the assistance of a team assigned specifically for this purpose.

The Instructional Intervention Team (IIT), sometimes also referred to as the Student Support Team or Teacher Assistance Team, is a collaborative team assembled to identify CLD students whose learning and behavior needs are not being met within mainstream classrooms (including bilingual/ESL). The intent of an instructional intervention team is to identify and provide appropriate in-class intervention assistance. Its specific concern is appropriate and effective intervention in the mainstream classroom for learning and behavior needs due to acculturation, language or cultural differences, disabilities, or the interaction of all of these. At the end of a specific instructional-intervention team period, the team decides whether to proceed to a formal referral or to continue monitoring the student's responses to intervention.

The IIT process provides a collaborative framework for identifying, addressing, documenting, and monitoring this intensive intervention. Research has shown that intensive IIT intervention over at least six weeks will address 70% to 85% of the student's needs, particularly those directly related to cultural and language differences and acculturation (Baca & Cervantes, 2003). To address these concerns, each school and school district should establish an IIT drawn primarily from regular and bilingual education personnel in the building. The first task of the collaborative team is to collect preliminary sociocultural and educational information about the student in question and then to identify appropriate interventions. The team will also assist the classroom teacher with implementing the interventions and monitoring the student's response to the interventions. Depending on the student's response, the team will then make a decision about alternate educational processes. There are five steps to the instructional intervention team process:

1.  Establish and nurture monitored intervention teams

2.  Identify and intervene for specific sociocultural factors

3. Identify and intervene for level and rate of acculturation

4. Identify and intervene for level, areas, and rate of language development and acquisition

5. Monitor and document the problem-solving process and response to interventions for a fixed period of time

Mainstream education personnel, including bilingual and ELL teachers, form the instructional intervention team within the building. The IIT members should be knowledgeable in a range of areas, including the following:

- Regular curriculum environment
- Cognitive/learning style and classroom performance
- Performance outside of academic settings
- Ethnic and linguistic community
- Family and community environment
- Interventions for specific behavior and learning needs
- Cross-cultural and cross-lingual learning
- Interventions for culture shock and acculturation
- Second language learning
- Interventions for cognitive language development

The most efficient configuration is a core of four or five teachers who meet on a weekly basis to consider new issues, plan interventions, or monitor ongoing student concerns. Joining them may be a number of other education professionals with special knowledge or skills that are useful in the particular student case under discussion. Thus, the weekly meeting may have from four to ten members present. The site based management team or its equivalent, working in conjunction with the school principal, may select the IIT members. Some schools have instructional intervention team members elected by the teaching staff.

In order to determine the student's needs, the instructional intervention team needs to gather and analyze all appropriate background data on the student. This includes a comprehensive profile of the student's culture and language background, experience, sociolinguistic development, acculturation level, and cognitive learning style. The instructional intervention team file contains this information, using either forms developed specifically for this purpose or general, district-developed forms.

Educators gather the information at this step in a variety of settings, both inside and outside of the classroom, including on the playground, during lunch, and outside of school, as appropriate. Information gathering may be through observation, interview, work samples, analytic teaching, portfolios, and classroom informal or other normal performance measures used within mainstream classrooms.

Some specific areas that need to be screened and monitored during the beginning two levels of the PRISIM process include the following: culture and language background, prior experience, cognitive learning style, sociolinguistic development, and acculturation level.

# CULTURE AND LANGUAGE

A student's cultural and linguistic background needs to be addressed by the instructional intervention team because the components of culture change continually and vary considerably from family to family, thus causing the linguistic and cultural background of the CLD student not always to be clear. The IIT will thus need to develop local *ethnologies*, comparative and analytical studies of the cultural and linguistic communities the school serves, which can be accomplished through the use of structured interviews and planned observations. Local institutions of higher education, churches, or other community organizations serving the CLD community may also be sources of information. This can be a district-supported activity, with the results maintained and disseminated via resource manuals throughout the district.

# COGNITIVE LEARNING STYLE

The instructional intervention team must analyze the CLD student's learning style in comparison to his or her teacher's teaching style to determine the degree of congruence or dissonance that is present. If the IIT identifies significant divergence between the CLD student's learning style and the teaching style of the classroom, interventions in cognitive learning strategies are appropriate and effective. The IIT may use inventory or other assessment tools to identify and compare learning and teaching styles.

# EXPERIENCE

The CLD student may lack appropriate responses to commonly used instructional strategies, which could compound their learning and behavior needs and may be mistaken as an indication of a disability. Some of the CLD students' responses to the school environment may be due to previous school experiences and others to linguistic or cultural differences. The instructional intervention team must sort out the effect of experience on student performance. One of the ways the IIT can implement this part of its information gathering is to interview parents or siblings about prior school experiences. Students who have been in school systems in other countries generally know basic school procedures, such as raising their hands for attention, asking permission to do something, and recess and lunchroom behaviors. However, they may be unfamiliar with particular instructional strategies common in US American public schools, such as independent or silent reading rather than group recitation or discovery learning rather than rote memorization.

# SOCIOLINGUISTIC DEVELOPMENT

As mentioned in Step 1, language is the primary medium through which culture and experiences are shared and transmitted from generation to generation, and it is a primary element in the acculturation of CLD students, especially those who are ELL or LEP. It is important to identify and assess the ELL and LEP student's sociolinguistic abilities in both first and second language because misunderstandings about these abilities are frequently involved in referrals. The identification of ELL and LEP students as language disabled when they exhibit auditory perception and expressive problems in English conflicts with the provisions of the reauthorized IDEA and other legislation and litigation. Only if ELL and LEP students demonstrate receptive and expressive language problems both in their native language and in English can they be said to have a linguistic disability. Thus, both English and native sociolinguistic development must be evaluated during the assessment process. Language assessment materials should reflect authentic classroom demands to the extent possible and should assess language in a functional context. This assessment will assist in determining if an ELL or LEP student has second language acquisition needs that have not been addressed. This assessment will also assist with culturally diverse students who appear to speak only English but are known to come from a home where a language other than English is spoken. Educators must gather language use information in a variety of contexts (for example, through observation of casual conversation with peers, interviews with the student, and tests) and provide information about both the social language and the academic language skills of the student.

ELL and LEP students' scores on norm referenced instruments in English and their native language must be carefully reviewed prior to making an evaluation for special placement. If the scores indicate limited native language skills as well as limited skills in English, the testing must be done in the native language first and then in English. Congruent performance would clearly justify the classification, while divergent performance would indicate unmet language needs.

## ACCULTURATION

It is evident from a review of previous research that the interrelationship of cultural and educational characteristics is central to answering questions about appropriate identification, referral, and instruction of culturally and linguistically diverse exceptional (CLDE) children (Baca & Cervantes, 2003; Finn, 1982; Ortiz & Yates, 1984; Rueda, 1985). It is also evident from these studies that the results of acculturation research have not been considered in this interrelationship, even though they could contribute to a better understanding of the issues related to the education of CLD students (Rogler, Cortes, & Malgady, 1991). The usefulness of acculturation theory and the measurement of acculturation for education personnel has been well established (Atkinson, Morten, & Sue, 1998).

The common image for acculturation is that of the melting pot, the complete assimilation of one group into another. Assimilation occurs when the native culture is essentially eliminated from the person's cognitive behavior as the second culture takes its place. However, this particular acculturative response is rather rare; a person more frequently integrates new cultural patterns into the cognitive and behavioral framework of the first culture. For example, a newcomer might assimilate in the sense that he or she learns and uses English in most communication situations while still retaining the habits and speech patterns that reflect the heritage language(s) and customs. As insinuated by the example, complete assimilation is only one of the possible results of the complex process of culture change known as acculturation, which is broadly described as the process of adapting to a new cultural environment.

Acculturation has been defined and redefined many times during the last seven decades. In 1936, Redfield, Linton, and Herskovits defined it thus: "Acculturation comprehends those phenomena which result when groups of individuals sharing different cultures come into continuous first-hand contact, with subsequent changes in the original culture patterns of either or both groups" (p. 149). Four decades later, Szapocznik, Scopetta, Kurtines, and Aranalde (1978) proposed that acculturation involves changes in two dimensions: behaviors and values. According to Szapocznik et al., the behavioral dimension of acculturation includes language use and participation in other cultural activities, and the values dimension reflects relational style, person-nature relationships, beliefs about human nature, and time orientation. In 1980, Padilla further expanded this understanding of acculturation by suggesting that this process also includes cultural awareness and ethnic loyalty. Cuellar, Arnold, & Maldonado (1995) defined acculturation in terms of changes at three levels of functioning: behavioral, affective, and cognitive. These encompass language, cultural mores and expressions, and emotions that have cultural connections.

Although most social scientists agree that every contact between cultures involves some degree of social and cultural integration, there are several ways to look at what happens during this contact and integration process. Before one can understand the dynamic process of culture change, one must first consider what is changing. *Culture* is a very broad and complex term and is usually viewed as a shared concept of reality or patterns of interaction, communication, and socialization held in common by a particular group of people. As employed in this discussion, culture is a cognitive construct; it is whatever one has to know or believe in order to operate in a manner acceptable to members of a certain group. It is not a material phenomenon. Culture, itself, is dynamic and no two individual members of the cultural group share exactly the same system of cultural knowledge. Some education professionals may express interest in other people's cultures while regretting that they do not have "a culture." If this is the case, they must first come to understand the impact of culture on their own lives prior to working with the impact of culture on the lives of others. All human beings are raised within a cultural context.

As a result of sharing behavioral patterns and values, each group of people has a common sense of cultural identity, and there is an identifiable boundary between members and nonmembers of the particular group. Some cultural characteristics are identifiable by both members and nonmembers of the group; for example, fluency in the Navajo language would be recognized as one possible indicator of Navajo-ness. However, some characteristics are not identifiable by nonmembers, such as recognizing the lack of speculation as a Navajo trait. Traditional Navajos rarely speculate about motives or past or future happenings. They generally report exactly what they see and hear without interpretation. In a study by Henry (1947), Hopi and Navajo children were asked to make up stories about a set of ambiguous pictures. The Navajos described what they saw and did not try to explain the pictured activity. The Hopi children explained what they thought the people were doing and why they were doing it. They also volunteered what they thought had led up to the activity and what might happen in the future. This different view of reality has implications in the use of particular curriculum materials or instructional techniques, or in the diagnosis of learning disabilities. For example, lack of apparent concern or speculation about past and future happenings is viewed in the United States as a normal child development stage passed at an early age and is used at times as an indicator of mental illness in older children and adults. However, as explained above, it is inappropriate to reach such conclusions about Navajo students when this has not been part of their cultural cognitive development.

As noted in Step 1, the process of learning a cultural context is called *enculturation*. Acculturation occurs when an enculturated individual comes into the proximity of a new or different culture. This may occur by moving into a new environment or location populated by people raised with a different language or culture, by going to a new school or moving to a new region of the country, or even through exposure to movies, television, and books that portray life in another culture. Just as goods and services may be exchanged by two cultures, so may values, languages, and behavior patterns. Padilla (1980) proposed that there are three stages of culture change: *contact, conflict,* and *adaptation.* He stated that any measurement of culture change must consider each of these three stages at both the group and individual level. The purpose of the contact must also be considered. The history, persistence, duration, purpose, and permanence of the contact, the nature of conflict and adaptations to this contact, as well as the individual's exposure to the second culture, interpersonal conflicts, and personal adaptations, are also important factors of consideration (Padilla, 1980). This includes examining the different adaptation patterns of "voluntary" and "involuntary minorities" (Ogbu & Simons, 1994). For example, voluntary minorities to the United States, such as Chinese immigrants, tend to be less concerned with prejudice and discrimination as opposed to involuntary minorities, such as African Americans. Where there is a deliberate extermination of beliefs over a long period of time, we find even greater culture change. There is almost always some degree of resistance to change because most cultural groups do not lightly give up valued practices, whether economic, religious, or communicative. This conflict can be manifested in many ways, such as psychological stress or physical aggression, but will always lead to some form of adaptation.

The dynamics of acculturation include selective adoption of the value system and the processes of integration and differentiation. This adaptation may take varied forms and the process of acculturation may be accompanied by some degree of shock, depending on how different the new situation is from that to which the individual is enculturated. This shock can vary from mildly uncomfortable to deeply disturbing, but it is a normal part of our adaptation to things that are new to us. On the mild end, all children who move frequently experience this culture shock whenever they must leave a school where they have made friends and know the teachers to attend a new school in a new community. On the extreme end, refugees can experience several different degrees of this psychological process when surviving and escaping imprisonment, adjusting to life in a refugee camp, and then immigrating to a new country unable to speak that country's language. There is a recognized pattern of response to acculturation, and those going through this culture shock may do so in a recurring cyclical manner. Educators who work with culturally and linguistically diverse students who have learning and behavior problems must address the effects of acculturation.

Another effect of culture change that is of key importance to educators is *acculturative stress.* This stress is common, though not inevitable, during culture change. Berry (1980) stated that acculturative stress is characterized by deviant behavior, psychosomatic symptoms, and feelings of marginality. He also found that variations in stress and culture change patterns were dependent to some extent upon the cultural and psychological characteristics of the culture group and the degree and nature of previous contact with culturally diverse groups. Berry observed that groups experience lower stress when their culture is more similar to the second culture or when they have had greater contact with other cultural groups. Students who consistently demonstrate heightened anxiety or stress, confused locus of control, or lack of response are often referred for special services since these are possible indicators of disabling conditions. Because of this, it is imperative that teachers working with CLD students who are experiencing acculturation consider the psychological side effects of acculturation in assessment and programming. Other side effects of acculturation include silence or withdrawal and distractibility, as well as code-switching and response fatigue (Schnell, 1996; Short & Porro-Salinas, 1996). Code-switching involves the insertion or substitution of sounds, words, syntax, grammar, or phrases from an existing language or communication process into the new, emerging language or communication process (C. Baker & Jones, 1998). Response fatigue occurs when the learner is overwhelmed and exhausted by new sights, sounds, movements, objects, and so on. Without a filter to distinguish important and critical stimuli from the unimportant, the individual must attend to everything. Appropriate placement for CLD students experiencing acculturative stress may be in cross-cultural counseling or acculturation assistance programs rather than in a special education program.

An additional result of culture change is emotional and substance abuse (Short & Porro-Salinas, 1996; Szapocznik & Kurtines, 1980). In Szapocznik and Kurtines' (1980) study, stress occurred when family members adjusting to life in mainstream US American culture did not integrate their home culture and language with that of the mainstream community. Although living in a community with two languages and cultures, parents and teenagers in the study rejected one culture and tried to identify exclusively with the other. These families were compared with families where parents and teenagers were bilingual and had developed cross-cultural methods of adapting to their new communities. The bilingual and cross-cultural families had fewer incidents of substance abuse and dysfunctional interactions than the monocultural families.

The Acculturation Matrix shown in Table 3 has quadrants that illustrate the four types of adaptation to the acculturative experience. It is based on models developed by Berry and his colleagues (Berry, Kim, Power, Young, & Bajaki, 1989).

In the upper left quadrant is *Assimilation.* As discussed previously, assimilation occurs when the home or heritage culture and language are completely replaced by the second or new language and culture. An example of this is the student who stops wearing traditional garb and adopts the clothing of his mainstream peers or who stops attending church with his family and converts wholly to the religion of some new group and regards that replacement as a positive aspect of his life. The educator should look for students who have completely substituted aspects from the mainstream for those in the home/heritage culture. Possible aspects include behaviors, words, and clothing.

**Table 3**  Acculturation Matrix

| Assimilation | Integration |
|---|---|
| Home culture and heritage language replaced by new culture and language | Home culture and heritage language blended with new culture and language |
| **Deculturation/Marginalization** | **Rejection** |
| Acceptance of neither home culture and heritage language nor new culture and language | Intentional rejection of home culture and heritage language for new culture and language<br>*or*<br>intentional rejection of new culture and language for that of home culture and heritage language |

In the upper right quadrant is *Integration.* In this box, one finds the ways in which a student has integrated language, behavior, clothing, food, religion, and other characteristic patterns from both the mainstream and the home/heritage cultures. An example is a student who is learning to speak English and uses it appropriately in responses while still speaking the heritage language with family and other members of the speech community, who dresses in US American style for school functions but wears appropriate garb for his or her family's religious activities, and who eats a hamburger and special ethnic dishes with equal pleasure.

The two quadrants on the top half of Table 3 are the positive adaptation responses to acculturation. The two quadrants on the bottom half are negative and destructive responses to acculturation. It is important to identify ways in which a student has one or both of the positive and negative elements so that appropriate interventions may be instituted. The lower right quadrant is *Rejection,* which is similar to assimilation in that it is essentially a monocultural response to acculturation, but it differs in its intent and impact. Rejection is when a person intentionally chooses to adhere to only one pattern of behavior and language. On the one hand, the person may reject the new culture and language situation and while living in this environment use only his or her home or heritage language, practicing only the traditional way of life, food, clothing, shelter, and so forth, with absolutely no attempt at integration. On the flip side, the person may intentionally reject all use of the home and heritage language and culture, trying to assimilate to the new environment forcibly by denying anything that is not part of the new situation or language. This state can be temporary, changing as the newcomer becomes more comfortable with the adopted country. Rejection is common in the case of refugees whose homelands were destroyed, particularly those traveling alone to the new country and with no hope of ever returning to their past situation. If no intervention is implemented, a state of rejection may cause serious, long-term psychological effects (Padilla, 1980). A family can be provided with specific strategies for working through this crisis and for restoring their child's comfort with being bilingual and bicultural. It is critical to respond with interventions for students who show rejection in either direction, as both are not healthy long-term responses to acculturation.

Of even more serious long-term impact on an individual is *Deculturation* or *Marginalization*. Deculturation is the loss of connection to the traditional, home, or heritage culture and language while not making the transition to the new culture or language. Marginalization represents the attitude of an individual with no interest in maintaining or acquiring proficiency in any culture, native or host. Both of these can result from not responding with effective interventions to rejection behaviors, but can also occur when children, students, or families are cut off from supportive community interactions within their home or heritage community and are not given assistance to transition into effective participation in the new language, culture, or community. Szapocznik and Kurtines (1980), discussing Mexican American adolescents, described gang affiliation and criminal behavior as possible results of this lack of supportive interactions. Indications of either deculturation or rejection are the priority areas for intervention and are indications of learning and behavior needs that must be addressed to reduce the degree of risk for the student.

In summary, major variables that affect acculturation include the amount of time spent in the process, the quantity and quality of interaction, ethnicity or nation of origin, and language proficiency. A review of the literature shows several critical factors identified as relating to success in acculturation:

- Presence of bilingual and English as a second language programs
- Strength in English language skills
- Strength in one or both first and second language skills
- Length of time in school
- Amount of interaction with mainstream US American students

Among the studies about these factors is Juffer's (1983) research on the importance of English language proficiency in determining degree of and success in acculturation. She found that English ability was significant in three of four subcategories and in predicting a high composite score on the adaptation inventory. Some of the research in bilingual education also indicates the importance of proficiency in the native language as a foundation for proficiency in second language acquisition and development, especially in the acculturation context. Cummins (1984) provided an extensive description of the relationship between L1 (first language) and L2 (second language) development and stressed the vital importance of L1 in promoting educational success and cognitive development in the diverse student in a cross-cultural learning situation. Szapocznik and Kurtines (1980) looked at the importance of strong language skills in both L1 and L2 as factors in mental health among linguistically diverse subjects. Juffer's (1983) study identified national origin as a factor that significantly predicted adaptation to a second culture. Her study also examined the relationship between degree of acculturation and length of time (1) in school and (2) in orientation to the acculturation experience. This study found that the degree of adaptation (acculturation) correlated highly with the length of time in school and orientation. Finn (1982) found that there were fewer referrals of ELL and LEP learners to special education in districts with bilingual programs. These studies all concluded that as bilingualism or biculturalism increases, socioemotional problems decrease, and they affirmed that bilingual education improves educational achievement for all of these culturally and linguistically diverse children.

Another factor Juffer (1983) identified as significant in acculturation was the amount of interaction with mainstream US American students. The number of CLD students enrolled in a school impacts the interactions between diverse and mainstream students. Finn (1982) indicated that there is a distinct relationship between CLD school enrollment and special education referral and placement. As CLD student enrollment in a school district increases, the referral and placement of culturally and linguistically diverse students to special education becomes more consistent with mainstream referral rates.

To recapitulate key points in the process of separating difference from disability, students who are in the process of adapting to a new culture or social environment may behave in a manner that is similar to a learning disability or other inhibiting factor. The evaluation of CLD students for eligibility in special education programs must include the assessment and consideration of these observable consequences of culture shock that may be confused with the commonly used criteria for learning or emotional disabilities. Where students are significantly less acculturated as measured on any of the various tools described in this and preceding sections, assessment and evaluation personnel must modify their evaluation procedures and choice of assessment tools to reflect the level of acculturation. The interpretation of evaluation findings must include discussion of the impact of the students' level and rate of acculturation as a factor contributing to all evaluation findings. This will help optimize the allocation of limited resources within the school and the district while providing each student with the most appropriate assistance.

In conclusion, at PRISIM Step 3 Tier 2, the focus should be on identifying and addressing emerging learning and behavior problems while continuing to support the CLD learner's access and achievement within the comprehensive core curriculum. This is best done through instructional intervention and continuing and expanding the differentiation of instruction within content areas. Problem solving and progress monitoring become even more important elements of the instructional intervention process at this step of separating difference from disability.

# JOSÉ CASE STUDY

## PRISIM Step 3 Intervention at Tier 2

After a year and a half in the school, José's classroom teacher, bilingual aide, and ELL teacher were all becoming concerned about his learning and behavior. In the classroom, he seemed distracted and not very attentive. He did not always respond when spoken to, although the teacher was sure he was capable of doing so. He now seemed to struggle with new content and was not making any progress with reading and writing in English. Up until now, José had always made an effort to be involved in whatever was going on in the classroom and on the playground. However, his behavior had started to deteriorate, and he had started getting into trouble and not paying attention. He had thrown a few temper tantrums when asked to complete tasks. His parents reported that he was refusing to speak Quechua at home and that he had expressed frustration when the family used their limited Spanish.

José appeared to have difficulty with task analysis and identifying the separate elements of assignments in detail. He was very resistant to change and did not respond well to storytelling time. He was very quick to respond to questions, but the answers seemed impulsive and random. He gave up readily, was easily distracted, and quite unstructured. When faced with new materials, José appeared particularly distressed and did not respond well to pressure. José seemed to leap to conclusions and make very broad generalizations. José responded best to physical demonstrations and concrete models.

Although José came to school every day and was not generally late getting back to classes after recess and lunch, his behavior in class had started to deteriorate, and he had begun acting out, fidgeting, and not paying attention. The playground monitor was afraid he had started hanging out with a group of gang wannabes during lunchtime and no longer played team sports with his classroom peers. His parents reported that José was sometimes acting up at home and not listening to his grandmother. José refused to speak Quechua with his grandmother and was starting to use bad words when he was frustrated.

## Needs Prioritization

The instructional intervention team completed a needs prioritization checklist to assist in simultaneously addressing José's emerging learning and behavior needs while continuing progress in language acquisition. They worked to facilitate and accelerate his acculturation, and support his retention of Spanish as a communication transfer bridge. Figure 15 illustrates the needs prioritization checklist done on José by the team. The three top areas identified on the team's checklist as needing intervention were acculturation, cognitive learning, and sociolinguistic development.

1. A second Acculturation Quick Screen was administered, and this time José received an AQS of 21.5. This means that after almost two years in the school, José is on the cusp between *less acculturated* and *in transition*. His rate of acculturation is slightly below normal.

2. A cognitive learning style inventory was completed, and it was found that José had a pattern of cognitive learning that was significantly different from and in dissonance with the teacher's instructional style. He was easily frustrated and showed low perseverance in completing tasks. He used several learning strategies that were not appropriate in the classroom. He also displayed difficulty with task analysis and understanding and applying cause and effect. These difficulties were particularly apparent during language arts and reading comprehension activities.

3. José's oral proficiency scores were 2 in English and 4 in Spanish after nearly two years of pull-out bilingual/ESL classes consisting of at least one hour per day every day of the week. His classroom teacher had administered classroom language inventories and said that his basic survival English was OK, but that he was not doing well with cognitive academic interactions. The ESL teacher, who was bilingual, said this was also true of his language interactions in Spanish. José's scores on a comprehensive cognitive academic language test in English were a 2 and a 3 in Spanish, confirming that José's English was now at the high end of the speech emergent level and his Spanish was at the intermediate level.

It was determined that the top need to address at this time was his deteriorating approach to content learning, followed by his adaptive behavior. Keeping up his English and supporting his Spanish were identified as important but not as critical as the impact of his general cognitive learning. However, when completing the needs identification checklist, it was discovered that José showed considerable difficulty with employing consistent and specific cognitive learning strategies. This led the team to monitor his use of learning strategies during the sheltered instruction and role-play activities. If José did not display consistent and effective learning strategies and show improvement in his retention and application of content, the team would make provisions to address this in more intensive settings.

## PRISIM 3 Tier 2 Intervention: Acculturation

The team reassessed José's level of acculturation and calculated his rate of acculturation to see if it was proceeding at a normal rate. Figure 16 is an excerpt from his AQS form. The instructional intervention team decided to implement a number of strategies to address José's level and rate of acculturation. These were role plays of using school culture and language and BICS/CALP (Magos & Politi, 2008; Rymes, Cahnmann-Taylor, & Souto-Manning, 2008; Webster-Stratton & Reid, 2008) and sheltered instruction (Echevarria, Vogt, & Short, 2004; Gibbons, 2002; Hansen-Thomas, 2008). They also began using more intensive strategies of consistent sequence (Vaughn & Linan-Thompson, 2007), and they started working with José on using self-monitoring techniques (Strickland, Ganske, & Monroe, 2002; Tomlinson, 1999). A progress monitoring spreadsheet was added to José's cumulative folder, in which each education professional working with José could make notes and indicate his level of achievement within each area.

## PRISIM 3 Tier 2 Intervention: Cognitive Learning

The instructional intervention team decided to implement a number of strategies to address José's cognitive learning style and his acquisition of effective learning strategies within the content areas. The first strategy employed in this intervention was to use advanced organizers in conjunction with José's writing and math lessons (Heacox, 2002; Moore, Alvermann, & Hinchmann, 2000; Opitz, 1998). This was expanded to other content when possible. The team also had a bilingual paraprofessional work with José on test-taking strategies (DeVries Guth & Stephens Pettengill, 2005; Hughes, Deshler, Ruhl, & Schumaker, 1993; Lebzelter & Nowacek, 1999). In math and social studies readings, the IIT assisted the classroom teacher in implementing active processing within small group work among José and peers (Cole 1995; Law & Eckes, 2000; Tovani, 2000) and during math activities, José was shown options for how to organize his data (Lapp, Flood, Brock, & Fisher, 2007; Moore et al., 2000). On the progress-monitoring spreadsheet added to José's cumulative folder, each education professional working with him could make notes and indicate his level of achievement within each content area.

## PRISIM 3 Tier 2 Intervention: Language

The team analyzed Jose's rate of acquisition of English and Spanish by comparing his proficiency scores at enrollment to his current performance. Figure 17 illustrates one of the informal inventories that was done of José's use of English in the classroom, in addition to his scores on the Woodcock Munoz in English and Spanish. Seeing that José went from Preproduction to Speech Emergence in 20 months on the Language Acquisition Grid (Table 1, from Chapter 2), the team concluded that his English was proceeding at a normal rate of acquisition, while his proficiency in his second language, Spanish, was slowing down a little. No specific alteration in ESL services was recommended at this time, other than to continue giving him direct instruction in English at least one hour per day every day of the week. It was also determined to increase José's access to Spanish language reading material appropriate to his reading level (2nd grade) by adding books to the school library.

| Sociocultural Factors | ☑ | Selected Cross-Cultural Adaptation Risk Factors |
|---|---|---|
| Acculturation Level | ✓ | Recent immigrant, refugee, migrant, or resident of a reservation |
| | | Does not interact much with majority culture peers or majority cultural group |
| | ✓ | Displays confusion in locus of control |
| | .5 | Displays heightened stress or anxiety in cross-cultural interactions |
| | ✓ | Oral expression contains considerable code switching |
| % Checked: **75%** | ✓ | Expresses or displays sense of isolation or alienation in cross-cultural interactions |
| | 4.5 | Out of 6 Total |
| Cognitive Learning Style | | Few cognitive learning strategies appropriate to classroom/school |
| | ✓ | Cognitive learning style different or inappropriate in relation to teacher's instructional style |
| | ✓ | Easily frustrated or low perseverance in completing tasks |
| | ✓ | Retains learning strategies that are no longer appropriate |
| % Checked: **83%** | ✓ | Displays difficulty with task analysis |
| | ✓ | Displays difficulty with understanding and applying cause and effect |
| | 5 | Out of 6 Total |
| Culture & Language | ✓ | Comes from non-English speaking home |
| | ✓ | Comes from a culture or ethnic group different from mainstream America |
| | ✓ | Family emphasizes support of family or community/group over individual effort |
| | ✓ | Comes from non-English speaking geographic area |
| % Checked: **83%** | | Has culturally appropriate behaviors that are different from expectations of mainstream |
| | ✓ | No support in the home for bilingual and bicultural development |
| | 5 | Out of 6 Total |
| Experiential Background | ✓ | High family mobility |
| | ✓ | Limited or sporadic school attendance |
| | ✓ | Low socioeconomic status |
| | ✓ | Little exposure to subject or content or not familiar with material |

*(Continued)*

**Figure 15** (Continued)

| Sociocultural Factors | ☑ | Selected Cross-Cultural Adaptation Risk Factors |
|---|---|---|
| | | Disrupted early childhood development |
| | | Few readiness skills |
| | | Does not know how to behave in classroom |
| % Checked: **44%** | | Different terms/concepts for subject areas or materials and content |
| | | Uses survival strategies that are not appropriate in the classroom |
| | 4 | Out of 9 Total |
| | | Does not speak English |
| Sociolinguistic Development | ✓ | Limited academic language in native language |
| | ✓ | Limited social language in English |
| | | Rarely speaks in class |
| | | Speaks only to cultural peers |
| % Checked: **63%** | ✓ | Limited academic language in English |
| | ✓ | Asks a peer for assistance in understanding |
| | ✓ | Appears to know English but cannot follow English directions in class |
| | 5 | Out of 8 Total |

**Figure 15**    Excerpt From Sociocultural Need Checklist for José After Eighteen Months

| Cultural/Environmental Factors | Information | Scores |
|---|---|---|
| 1. Number of years in United States/Canada | About two years | 1.5 |
| 2. Amount of time in school district | 180 × 12 = 2,160 good attendance | 2 |
| 3. Amount of time in ESL/bilingual education | 180 × 1.25hr × 2 = 450 | 2 |
| 4. Native language proficiency | Quechua BICS | 3 |
| 5. English language proficiency | SOLOM 13, CLIC 15 | 2.5 |
| 6. Bilingual proficiency | Quechua, Spanish, some English | 3 |
| 7. Ethnicity/nation of origin | Quechua, Peru | 1.5 |
| 8. % in school speaking student's language/dialect | 1% Quechua | 6 |
| | **AQS Score Total:** | 21.5 |

**Figure 16**    Excerpt From Second Acculturation Quick Screen Results for José After Eighteen Months

| SOCIAL CLASSROOM | Native Language | | English |
|---|---|---|---|
| 1. Follows general directions (Spanish & Quechua) | ✓ | ✓ | ✓ |
| 2. Acts out common school activities | ✓ | ✓ | ✓ |
| 3. Points, draws, or gestures responses | ✓ | ✓ | ✓ |
| 4. Verbalizes key words | ✓ | ✓ | ✓ |
| 5. Gives commands to peers | ✓ | ✓ | ✓ |
| 6. Exchanges common greetings | ✓ | ✓ | ✓ |
| 7. Uses limited vocabulary | ✓ | ✓ | ✓ |
| 8. Describes objects; describes people | ✓ | ✓ | ✓ |
| 9. Retells a familiar story | ✓ | ✓ | ✓ |
| 10. Initiates and responds to a conversation | ✓ | ✓ | ✓ |
| 11. Appears to attend to what is going on | ✓ | ✓ | ✓ |
| 12. Appropriately answers basic questions | ✓ | ✓ | ✓ |
| 13. Participates in sharing time | ✓ | ✓ | |
| 14. Narrates a simple story | ✓ | ✓ | |
| 15. Between 1,000–6,000 receptive vocabulary | ✓ | ✓ | ✓ |
| **Total social classroom interactions used in classroom** | 15 | 15 | 13 |
| **Total possible social classroom interactions** | | 15 | 15 |

| ACADEMIC CLASSROOM | Spanish | English |
|---|---|---|
| 16. Follows specific directions for academic task | ✓ | ✓ |
| 17. Follows along during oral reading | ✓ | ✓ |
| 18. Understands teacher's discussion | ✓ | |
| 19. Uses sound/symbol association | ✓ | |
| 20. Decodes words | ✓ | |
| 21. Generates simple sentences | ✓ | ✓ |
| 22. Completes simple unfinished sentences | ✓ | |
| 23. Makes some pronunciation and basic grammatical errors but is understood | ✓ | ✓ |
| 24. Asks for clarification during academic tasks | ✓ | |
| 25. Asks/answers specific questions regarding topic | ✓ | ✓ |
| 26. Actively participates in class discussions; volunteers to answer questions | | |
| 27. Responds orally and in written form | | |
| 28. Can explain simple instructional tasks to peers | ✓ | |
| 29. Adds an appropriate ending after listening to a story | | |
| 30. Initiates conversations and questions | ✓ | ✓ |
| 31. Demonstrates an interest in reading | | |
| 32. Understands and uses temporal and spatial concepts | ✓ | |
| 33. Distinguishes main ideas from supporting details | | |
| 34. Understands rules of punctuation and capitalization for reading | | |
| 35. Engage in and produce connected narrative | ✓ | |

*(Continued)*

**Figure 17** (Continued)

| | | |
|---|---|---|
| 36. Can communicate thoughts | ✓ | |
| 37. Makes complex grammatical errors | | |
| 38. Writes from dictation | | |
| 39. Understands and uses academic vocabulary appropriately | | |
| 40. Reads for comprehension | | |
| 41. Can discuss vocabulary | | |
| 42. Uses glossary, index, appendix, and so on | | |
| 43. Uses expanded vocabulary | | |
| 44. Functions on academic level with peers | | |
| 45. Maintains two-way conversation | ✓ | |
| | | |
| **Total academic language interactions used in classroom** | 16 | 6 |
| **Total possible academic language interactions** | 40 | 40 |
| **Total classroom language interactions used in classroom** | 31 | 19 |
| **Total possible classroom language interactions** | 55 | 55 |

**Figure 17**   Excerpt From Jose's Second Classroom Language Interaction Checklist, After 18 Months

# Intensive Intervention and Progress Monitoring $4$

**PRISIM Step 4. Intensive Intervention and Progress Monitoring**

*Designing and implementing an intensive instructional intervention plan with specifically targeted progress monitoring to determine the student's response to intervention. Implementing a sequence of specific individualized interventions to identify the capacity of a CLD learner to participate effectively in your school's programs. Identifying specific areas of concern in the CLD student's response to intervention that warrant further evaluation and monitoring. In programs using the tiered RTI or RTII model, this step coincides with Tier 3.*

Current RTI and RTII models are based on three or four tiers. Usually, in all models at Tier 1, general education teachers provide instruction within the core curriculum to all students in the school. It is assumed that approximately 80% of students will be successful within the school's Tier 1 benchmarked curriculum and will not need additional intensive assistance. Some three tier models include differentiated learning environments as part of Tier 1. In four tier models, specific differentiation for learning and behavior, particularly language transition and behavior adaptation support for students experiencing culture shock, is provided within Tier 1 and continued into the other tiers as necessary. In both three- and four-tier models, Tier 2 is generally focused, small group assistance, while within Tier 3, more individualized, one-on-one, target interventions are implemented. Reading specialists, ESL instructors, and content area assistance may be provided to struggling students at Tier 2 in small group pullout, plug-in, or push-in situations or at Tier 3 in one-to-one interactions.

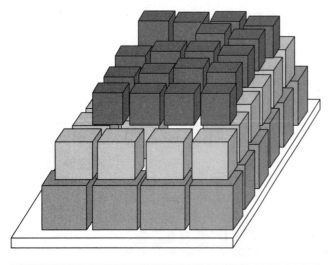

**Figure 18** Adding a layer of individualized intensive intervention to the PRISIM pyramid

When students fail to respond to small group, Tier 2-type interventions or intense individualized interventions that are typical at Tier 3, they may be moved into an individualized program at Tier 4 that is specially designed to meet their unique needs. In all problem-solving models, including RTI and RTII systems, CLD students can be referred for special education at any point that it is determined that their learning and behavior problems are not due to cultural or linguistic differences and are beyond the capacity of general education personnel alone. Success is achieved when diverse learners are able to participate effectively at or near peers in all programs and content areas and to sustain learning within a differentiated general program.

All teachers may help to develop interventions and plan assessments for students receiving instruction and interventions in Tiers 1 and 2; however, special education personnel generally do not provide instruction to students until Tier 3 or 4, when the student is receiving the most individualized and intensive level of instruction and intervention. Tier 4 usually includes CLD students in specially designed, integrated, individualized instructional programs; on individualized education plans; and with other special education or related service provisions.

## THE PROGRESSION OF INTERVENTIONS

A teacher may end up using all of the strategies represented by the shaded blocks in Figure 18, but might differentiate them for individual CLD students' needs and issues. For example, the teacher will use strength-based strategies at Tier 1. These strategies will be comprehensive, differentiated, generally geared to the larger group process, and based on the strengths and resiliencies of his or her students. If the teacher notices that some CLD students need more differentiation of instruction, he or she will move to an even more focused strategy set at Tier 2 and implement intensive interventions in small group or paired settings for particular students. Many different approaches may be used at this level, and many will be successful for the majority of the CLD students. However, some students will need even more individualization, and some students will require problem solving and assistance from other education personnel. If this is the case, the teacher will move the student into a Tier 3 mode of problem solving. At Tier 3, the student is more tightly monitored and more intensity is used in individual interventions. During this intensive RTI or RTII Tier 3 process, it is extremely important that specific cultural and linguistic issues continue to be addressed, as well as the specific learning and behavior issues that are part of the teacher's concern. Under the reauthorized IDEA of

2004, before school personnel can move to full and individual evaluation (FIE) and consider placement in special education services, the team must document the extent to which language and culture issues are part of the presenting problem and demonstrate that they are not the most significant determining factor. Following are specific language and culture questions that must be addressed during the problem solving process.

## ASKING THE RIGHT QUESTIONS

Language and culture issues frequently appear in school settings as questions asked by concerned school personnel, such as "He has been here over two years, so isn't his lack of academic achievement a sign of a possible disability?" or "She was born here, so can't we rule out culture shock and language development issues?" Although illustrative of good intentions and heartfelt concern for these students, it is more productive to ask what information is still needed and how it will be used. The information to be gathered will answer specific questions that are critical to separating difference from disability.

> **Education:** Has the student been in school before? Are there gaps in the student's education experiences? Has the student had sufficient intensity of instruction?
>
> **Home language**: Are languages other than English spoken in the student's home? What languages other than English does the student speak? Is the student maintaining an ability to communicate with his or her family members?
>
> **Language proficiency**: What is the student's language proficiency and literacy? Is the student developing the home language at a normal rate?
>
> **English**: Does the student need assistance with learning English? Is the student acquiring English at a normal rate?
>
> **Achievement:** What is the student's level and rate of academic achievement? Is this normal for the general student population in your district or school? What about for the specific cultural population of the student?
>
> **Behavior**: Is the student's emotional stability developmentally and culturally appropriate? Are there individual or family circumstances that may explain the observed behavior?
>
> **Adaptation:** What is the student's level of acculturation? Is the student at risk for culture shock? Is the student adapting to the school at a normal rate?

## HOW TO USE THE INFORMATION

Information about students is not valuable if it is not instructionally meaningful and does not lead to a course of action for the student's benefit.

**Education:** Prior experience in school, whether in the United States or another country, facilitates transitional instructional models. Knowing that the student has received schooling elsewhere tells school personnel that they can focus on the transition from an academic language foundation to English academic language. If the student has never had a formal education experience, school personnel must start by building an understanding of school culture, rules, expectations, and basic school interaction language in the student's most proficient language before transitioning into English.

Separating difference from disability concern: If the student shows little progress in adapting to school expectations and continues to struggle with acquiring school interaction language in his or her home language, there may be an undiagnosed disability and the student should be referred for a full evaluation.

**Home language:** Students who are raised in homes where English is used infrequently or is only one of many languages used in the home come to school with unique strengths that can become the foundation of instruction. Research shows that they have cognitive and linguistic capacities that can facilitate learning (Kovelman & Petitto, 2002). In addition, psychological well-being is built on quality family communication and interactions.

Separating difference from disability concern: If the student has not acquired a developmentally appropriate proficiency in a language other than English, it may be due to family circumstances (see discussion under behavior and adaptation) or the presence of an undiagnosed disability. In either case, this can delay English acquisition. A structured intensive intervention (part of an RTI/RTII) in the primary home language would show whether the student has the ability to develop language and communication to an acceptable level. If the student's communication does not improve under intervention, then a referral for a full evaluation would be warranted.

**Language and literacy:** The student's proficiency and background in a language other than English assists in deciding on the most effective instructional communicative models. It is critical to assess, to the extent possible, the student's proficiency in his or her home language and communication mode. Since standardized tests are not available for every language or communication mode, alternative measures are frequently needed. These can be structured sampling and observation, interview, interactive inventories, and other analytic tools. Rubrics for interpreting these tools are also available.

Separating difference from disability concern: A student may score low on a standardized test in his or her home language because the student has never received instruction in the language and has only an oral proficiency. Thus, low primary language and low English may look like there is some language disability. A structured intensive intervention in the primary language, including basic phonics and literacy readiness, would serve two purposes: (1) It would profile the student's proficiency, and (2) it would establish whether the low score is learning-based rather than something else. If the student makes little or no progress in the RTI/RTII, a referral for a full evaluation is necessary.

**Communication:** The student's language proficiency in English is directly related to eligibility for and the entry level of instruction in English as a second language. There are many tools available for determining whether a student needs assistance with learning English. For initial services in English language learning for limited English proficient speakers (ELL/LEP), school personnel should select instruments that are quick, unbiased, and that focus on speaking and listening skills. Including a literacy screening would be instructionally meaningful only for students who have received prior instruction in English.

Separating difference from disability concern: Some students speak enough English to not qualify for ELL or LEP services, but have such a limited classroom language foundation that they look like students with learning disabilities. Thus, English screening for ELL and LEP services must include screening for cognitive academic language proficiency (CALP), not just social language (BICS). If the student is ELL or LEP and is also receiving special education services for a disability, the IEP must list the ELL and LEP accommodations as part of the related services. This could be bilingual assistance, or specially designed academic instruction in English (SDAIE) within the special education setting, or some other appropriate monitored intervention with specific objectives related to acquiring English. SDAIE classes are for students with intermediate to advanced levels of English proficiency and grade-level academic development in their primary language. The focus of SDAIE classes is on academic content, which is taught using special techniques to make instruction comprehensible. Accommodations, such as those listed previously, often involve adapting language (spoken or written) to make it more understandable to second language learners. During assessment, accommodations may be made in the presentation, response method, setting, or timing and scheduling of the assessment. In many cases, the disabling condition is such that it seriously impacts the acquisition of English, and thus, special education personnel and ELL/LEP personnel must work together on realistic outcomes.

**Cognitive:** All children can learn, but they learn at different rates and in different manners. A challenge of today's standards-based education models is that students who do not fit the scope and sequence of a particular school system are frequently placed in alternative instructional settings that may or may not be appropriate to their needs.

Separating difference from disability concern: If a student is not meeting the benchmarks established by a school system even when given learning support, he or she may be referred to special education as having a learning disability of some sort. Sometimes special education is the only instructional alternative available in the building; nevertheless, it is not appropriate to place students who do not have a disability into special education even when it is the best alternative instructional setting available. In this case, it is recommended to restructure all programs to include differentiated instructional environments where any student can enter a lesson at his or her entry point and learn to the maximum of his or her abilities. A structured intensive intervention in fundamental learning strategies would establish whether the low score is learning-based rather than something else. If the student makes little or no progress in the RTI/RTII, a referral for a full evaluation is necessary.

**Behavior:** Family and community events can be contributing factors to behavior problems, and it is critical to effective instruction to explore both school and nonschool environments and their relationship to the problem the student is presenting. Whether the behavior problem is due to an innate disorder, biochemical dysfunction, or a temporary response to trauma or disruption in the student's home or school environment, the student needs effective and immediate intervention and assistance.

Separating difference from disability concern: Although the student needs assistance with managing or controlling his or her behavior, special education is not the appropriate placement if the etiology of the problem is culture shock, a specific event, or chronic stressors in the student's home or school environment. An intensive instructional intervention that facilitates self-monitoring and control within a supportive and safe environment should always be implemented first. If the problem does not appear to decrease in frequency or intensity, or if the student makes little or no progress, a referral for a full evaluation is necessary.

**Adaptation:** The level and rate of acculturation, and accompanying degree of culture shock, must be addressed within the instructional environment. All students must adapt to the school environment, whether they speak English or not; students who come to school from homes or communities very different from the mainstream culture will experience a greater degree of culture shock.

Separating difference from disability concern: The manifestations of culture shock look a lot like learning and behavior disabilities, and unaddressed acculturation and adaptation needs can concatenate into serious learning and behavior problems later in the education experience. An intensive instructional intervention that mitigates culture shock and facilitates adaptation and language transition should be always be implemented, particularly for newcomers. Most students will respond within a few weeks to this intervention. This positive response to intervention does not guarantee that culture shock will not reappear because culture shock is cyclical and a normal part of our adaptation to anything unfamiliar to us. However, a positive response to acculturative assistance lets school personnel know that the presenting problems are due to a normal adaptive process, acculturation, which responds over time to instructional intervention. Students should have their level of acculturation measured at their entry into the school system, and their rate of acculturation should be monitored annually to assure that the students are making normal progress in school. If the student's rate of acculturation is not within the normal range, it is an indication either that the program is not adequately addressing his or her transition needs or that there may be an undiagnosed disability of some sort that is depressing the rate of acculturation.

Although RTI and RTII are generally thought of as referring to academic intervention, most programs (93.3% according to Berkeley, Bender, Peaster, & Saunders, 2009) also incorporate behavioral interventions or use a similar multitiered approach to address the behavioral needs of students. All but one of the programs examined by Berkeley et al. (2009) use tiered approaches to address behavior, in addition to academics. In conclusion, instructional intervention, RTI, and RTII are seen as a positive development in assisting all learners, including those with specific learning and behavior problems associated with diverse languages and backgrounds, and may be summarized as follows:

**Table 4**  What RTI/RTII for CLD Is and What It Is Not

| RTI/RTII for CLD IS | RTI/RTII for CLD IS NOT |
|---|---|
| An initiative that supports general education (inclusive of ELL services) school improvement goals for all diverse learners | A stand-alone special education initiative |
| Intended to help as many CLD and ELL students as possible meet proficiency standards without special education | A means for just getting more students into special education |
| A method to unify general, ELL, CLD, and special education in order to benefit CLD students through greater continuity of services | A method for solely increasing or decreasing the number of CLD students in special education |
| Focused primarily on effective, comprehensive, differentiated instruction to enhance CLD student growth | Focused primarily on learning disability determination among CLD students |
| A way of identifying and facilitating specific language and acculturation development among CLD students | A way of determining learning disabilities through a checklist |

# RESPONSE TO INTERVENTION PLAN FOR CLD STUDENTS

Within an average instructional intervention team period of eight to twelve weeks, several specific learning and behavior problems may be addressed. The instructional intervention team process usually takes at least six weeks, while the team observes and documents positive responses to each successive or concurrent intervention. The instructional intervention team designs an instructional intervention plan that specifies the responsibilities of each member to address the following:

   a. Any academic areas impacted by language difficulties

   b. Learning and behavior problems arising from culture shock

   c. Improvement of verbal skill in one or both languages

    d. Improvement of writing skill in one or both languages

    e. Any medical, behavioral, or emotional needs; adaptive behavior skills

    f. Any cognitive learning strategies that would enhance students' ability to engage in learning

    g. Community services needed and outside agencies to access (food, clothing, employment, protective services, counseling)

The plan should specify who will be responsible for implementing each of the interventions and in what order they will proceed, which should be based on their prioritization of the student's needs. In designing goals, one must make sure that all of them are specific, measurable, and achievable. A summary review date should be set for the plan (six to eight weeks away is suggested), and weekly meetings should be used to monitor the instructional intervention team process.

The team will use a focused planning and documentation process to record and monitor the intervention goals and interventions being implemented. These problem solving with progress monitoring models provide classroom personnel with lists of appropriate strategies and interventions that address specific learning and behavior problems and guidance in modifying and monitoring the language of instruction. Examples of appropriate interventions for RTI and RTII implementations include the following:

## Language Acquisition

Appropriate language acquisition interventions include content instruction in the first language, bilingual assistance in content areas, ESL, two-way bilingual instruction, and bilingual language and content area instruction. Sheltered English techniques, as well as sheltered instruction in both languages, are also an option. In the sheltered classroom, teachers use simplified language, physical activities, visual aids, and the environment to teach vocabulary for concept development in mathematics, science, social studies, and other subjects. Additional language and communicative areas that can be addressed in interventions are code switching, stages in second language acquisition, and development of social and academic language (BICS and CALP). Instruction and interventions must also involve *comprehensible input*, an explanation of language learning proposed by Krashen (1981) that states that language acquisition occurs when instruction is provided at a level that is comprehensible to the learner. This can be achieved by modeling, demonstration, physical and visual examples, guided practice, and other strategic instructional practices.

## Acculturation Needs

CLD students' needs for acculturation interventions is indicated by their performance on acculturation measures, such as the AQS, or based upon expert observation. Appropriate interventions that address acculturation needs and acculturative stress are those that address culture shock, resistance to change, distractibility, response fatigue, limited experience in academic settings, confusion in locus of control, stress reactions, and other psychological side-effects of the acculturation process. Appropriate interventions for addressing learning and behavior difficulties are included in the RTI/RTII and other sources. Among these interventions are the following:

- Cognitive Learning Assistance: Addresses cognitive learning differences between teaching style and the CLD student's cognitive learning style and other cognitive academic needs, such as academic language acquisition, metacognitive strategies, and cognitive learning strategies.
- Behavioral Assistance: Addresses distractibility, disorientation, confusion in locus of control, withdrawal, acting out, and other behaviors that may be manifestations of culture shock or side effects of the acculturation process.
- Ethno-Ecological Assistance: Addresses the adaptation needs of children within the family, school, and community through peer tutoring, cross-cultural communication strategies for both the CLD student and classmates, and increasing family and community involvement in the school program.

**Table 5**   Example Intervention Strategies for Learning and Behavior Difficulties for CLD

| | | |
|---|---|---|
| • Academic support services | • Consulted resource people | • Peer tutors |
| • Accelerated reading strategies | • Cooperative learning | • Planned positive reinforcement |
| • Acculturation support | • Counseling services | • Reduction of stimuli |
| • Adapted instructional materials | • Guided reading strategies | • Sheltered English instruction |
| • Affective strategies | • Guided writing strategies | • Suggestions for/from parents |
| • Behavioral contract | • Mentoring | • Support groups |
| • Bilingual materials | • Metacognitive assistance | • Varied content/strategies |
| • Bilingual reading recovery | • Parent conferences | • Varied instructional setting |
| • Cognitive learning strategies | • Parent/teacher team | • Varied outcomes |

The instructional intervention team advises the teacher or staff member about appropriate interventions and provides resources and guided practice in their implementation. Members of the team may go into the classroom and work directly with the student, may team teach with the teacher, may pull the student out to implement a specific strategy, or may otherwise become directly and collaboratively involved in implementing the recommended intervention for the culturally and linguistically diverse learner with learning and behavior problems. The instructional intervention team's active involvement also facilitates its monitoring of the student's response to the recommended interventions.

Interventions should not be chosen at random, but rather should be selected and implemented to target specific, identified learning and behavior problems that are of concern to the teacher. The educator should study the scores and data from the screening forms and refer to the guidelines for interpreting these results. Each screening form should have an administration manual that contains information about the tools, suggestions for intervention, and concern focus areas as they relate to CLD students. For each area of concern, interventions are identified and noted for the instructional setting, instructional strategies, content, and for student behaviors. For example, having a CLD student work in a small group (setting) assigned to work cooperatively on an inquiry activity (strategies) for a science project (content) will have a great impact on student behavior. This is particularly true if all members of the group speak the same language, such as Russian or Spanish, versus multiple languages. The setting, strategies, content, or behavior cannot be changed without addressing its interaction with the other three.

Strategies used within the instructional intervention RTI and RTII process must be as narrowly focused as possible to have the greatest impact on the learner and his or her learning or behavior problem. This *strategy fitness* is critical to implementing interventions with CLD students. Too often, school personnel are using packaged RTI materials designed for general reading or math problems among native English speakers. The intervention strategies may need extensive modification to be of benefit for CLD and limited English proficient students. One way to organize the modified implementation of a student's particular strategic intervention is to use the PEARL strategy framework (Collier, 2004b). This basic strategy for all diverse instruction is outlined in Figure 19 (Planning Sheet for PEARL). The acronym PEARL stands for the essential elements to be included in implementing specific strategies or instructions or interventions for limited English speaking students.

1. **PREVIEW** using comprehensible input strategies. Use prediction, preparation, preview, and general overview of what is to come in the lesson or activity.

2. **EMBED** in context-rich activities, including concrete, explicit structure or models and making sure that concrete context is used.

3. **ATTACH** to what has already been learned. Always connect learning to prior lessons and knowledge. Make intentional and overt connections between the new content or activity and things that are familiar to the learner, making meaningful attachments through analogies and illustrations between the known and the unknown.

4. **RATCHET** both the content and the context of the learning. Extend and build on what is learned like cogs in a gear mechanism. Enrich and expand upon learning, using skills in L1 to strengthen L2 learning and skills in L2 to strengthen L1.

5. **LOOK BACK** at what was learned and how learning occurred. Review content as well as the strategy used to learn. Have students reflect on what they have learned and how they will use this information, and discuss why the lesson was taught the way it was and what strategies facilitated their learning.

| Student's Name | | | | | | Homeroom Teacher | | | | |
|---|---|---|---|---|---|---|---|---|---|---|
| | | | | | | | | | | |

| Date of intervention | | | | | | Lesson | | | | |
|---|---|---|---|---|---|---|---|---|---|---|
| | | | | | | | | | | |
| | | | | | | | | | | |
| | | | | | | | | | | |

| **P** | Plan: |
|---|---|
| PREVIEW | Observation |

| | | | | | | | | | | |
|---|---|---|---|---|---|---|---|---|---|---|
| | | | | | | | | | | |

| **E** | Plan: |
|---|---|
| EMBED | Observation |

| | | | | | | | | | | |
|---|---|---|---|---|---|---|---|---|---|---|
| | | | | | | | | | | |

| **A** | Plan: |
|---|---|
| ATTACH | Observation |

| | | | | | | | | | | |
|---|---|---|---|---|---|---|---|---|---|---|
| | | | | | | | | | | |

| **R** | Plan: |
|---|---|
| RATCHET | Observation |

| | | | | | | | | | | |
|---|---|---|---|---|---|---|---|---|---|---|
| | | | | | | | | | | |

| **L** | Plan: |
|---|---|
| LOOK BACK | Observation |

| | | | | | | | | | | |
|---|---|---|---|---|---|---|---|---|---|---|
| | | | | | | | | | | |

**Figure 19**  Planning Sheet for PEARL

The instructional intervention team monitors and evaluates the implementation of each intervention for its effectiveness with a particular CLD student. The student's response to each intervention within the particular context and language in which it is carried out is recorded and the observed patterns are noted. For example, changing the composition of the peer team in which an ELL/LEP student is working (e.g., including two bilingual students who are proficient in the student's native language) may result in more consistent success in completing assignments. This would be done in a variety of subject areas, and its success or failure in producing differences in the student's behavior would be noted. It could indicate that the ELL/LEP student needs additional assistance with language acquisition and academic language in English, that the student feels more comfortable working with these peers, or it could mean something else entirely. The positive results achieved by the intervention are noted on the instructional intervention team documentation form.

During the instructional intervention period, it is especially important to document the contexts and content areas or approaches in which the CLD student is successful. These will be helpful in determining further interventions, in guiding the classroom teachers in successful modifications and adaptations, and in building up an accurate learning and behavior profile of the student. This information will also be useful to the evaluation team, should the instructional intervention team decide to refer the CLD student for an evaluation.

The decision to advance to another need area on the instructional intervention team's priority list may occur after two weeks, or possibly less. One intervenes for level, areas, and rate of language development and acquisition, and then one selects the next need on the priority list.

After at least six to eight weeks, but no longer than twelve, the team should reach a decision about exiting the student from the instructional intervention team process. There are two likely decisions at this point:

1. **The intervention succeeds and the student exits the intensive monitoring.** The student may continue to receive appropriate first language development and second language acquisition assistance.

2. **The team decides to refer the student for formal evaluation.** The instructional intervention team determines that the student's learning and behavior needs are *not* due to cultural or linguistic differences or that the student has some other learning or behavior need, in addition to learning and behavior needs related to second language acquisition, acculturation, and sociocultural adaptation. At this point, a formal referral to special education is justified and the student is exited from the intervention process.

The essence of the prevention and intervention step of the assessment paradigm is to determine the degree to which the student's sociocultural background is having an impact on his or her learning or behavior problem in the school and to determine if something other than the normal side effects of acculturation and second language acquisition are a factor.

In conclusion, PRISIM 4 is the point in the seven-step PRISIM process where more intensive intervention is implemented, similar to Tier 3 in RTI and RTII. The focus of this tier is assessing the capacity of the CLD student to respond to instruction and intervention, while at the same time identifying specific strategies that are effective in facilitating learning for the student. A summary of the elements that a district must address in, or before reaching, the intervention step includes:

1. Someone is concerned that a diverse learner has a learning or behavior problem.

2. A specific team of education professionals (e.g., the instructional intervention team) receives the initial inquiry for assistance and collaborates with concerned personnel about the student.

3. A specific process exists to collect and monitor information about the student's learning and behavior during the intervention period.

4. The prevention/intervention period should last from six to eight weeks.

5. Specific instruments or procedures exist to identify appropriate preventions (enhancements) and interventions for the student's level of acculturation, language, adaptive behavior, and other areas of concern.

6. Interventions for acculturation, language, and other aspects of adaptive behavior are implemented by classroom personnel.

7. Classroom personnel receive assistance from the instructional intervention team, or other designated collaborative consultants, in implementing the interventions and monitoring during the intervention period.

8. Documentation is kept about the prevention, interventions, and student responses to them.

9. This documentation is used to make a decision either to terminate or continue the intervention period.

Bender and Shores (2007) stated that in RTI and RTII models, this tier involves highly intensive, specifically targeted individual instruction with even more frequent progress monitoring that may include placement in special education. By asking the right questions, gathering the appropriate types of information about CLD students, and knowing how to apply that information in a way that is beneficial to CLD students academically and socially, one has the foundation for separating difference from disability and supplying students with the support they require.

# JOSÉ CASE STUDY

## Intervention at PRISIM Step 4

Although some of the instruction and interventions implemented at Steps 1, 2 and 3 were effective in improving José's learning and behavior, he was still struggling to adapt and achieve in some areas. He received Step 3 interventions in a pullout setting in a small group of ELL/LEP peers that addressed his culture shock, including role play, consistent sequence, sheltered instruction in reading and math, and other strategies. His English proficiency was progressing at a normal rate, and so no specific interventions were implemented aside from continuing to ensure that José received at least one hour of specific bilingual/ESL direct instruction every day of the week. The issue of retention of his L2 (Spanish) as a communication transfer bridge was addressed at Step 3 by increasing his access to Spanish language reading material in the school library.

After eight weeks of monitoring José's progress in Step 3 interventions, a second needs prioritization was done. While José showed progress with oral communication in English and Spanish, he continued to struggle with reading in all content areas and in both languages. According to his teachers and support staff, he appeared to be "stuck" at a third grade level in both languages. The team decided to add more intensive individualized interventions, continue to monitor José's progress, and determine if he had an undiagnosed learning disability of some sort.

## PRISIM 4 Tier 3 Intervention: Acculturation

The instructional intervention team implemented a number of strategies to address José's slower than normal rate of acculturation at an intensive individual level. They had all teaching staff go over task steps and scripts for consistent sequencing, as recommended by Vaughn & Linan-Thompson (2007). The IIT also had a bilingual aide work one-on-one with José in the use a self-monitoring checklist (Borba, 2001; Strickland et al., 2002). After demonstrating and reinforcing its use, the aide had José design his own checklist for attending to school rules for appropriate social interactions with teachers, staff, and peers. The progress monitoring spreadsheet in his cumulative folder was expanded to include individual monitoring.

## PRISIM 4 Tier 3 Intervention: Content Learning

The instructional intervention team implemented a number of strategies to address José's content learning and his reading comprehension within the content areas. They individualized José's use of advanced organizers in his writing and math lessons (Heacox, 2002). In math and social studies readings, José was shown how to preview and organize his data (Lapp et al., 2007; Moore et al., 2000). A bilingual aide showed José how to use a math word-problem solving strategy that walked him through the process and provided a mnemonic, SQRQCQ (Survey, Question, Reread, Question, Compute,

Question), to remember the process (Elliot & Thurlow, 2005). The reading specialist pulled José out and reviewed basic sound-symbol relationships for two weeks while the bilingual ESL teacher reviewed Spanish phonemes and highlighted similarities and differences between Spanish and English sounds and symbols for José. Math and social studies textbooks from Mexico were received from the Mexican Consul in the state capital. Spanish content textbooks in all content areas are available from the consulate and contain appropriate and parallel content that is acceptable to state guidelines (García, 2005; Kovelman, Baker, & Petitto, 2008). If José were older, the district has a CONEVyT (*Consejo Nacional de Educacion para la Vida y el Trabajo*, National Council for Lifelong Learning and Work Skills) portal (*Plazas Comunitarias*) and could have had him taking Mexican and state cross-accredited courses. The progress monitoring spreadsheet in his cumulative folder was expanded to include individual monitoring.

## PRISIM 4 Tier 3 Intervention: Language

José was proceeding at a normal rate of acquisition in English, his third language, while his proficiency in his second language, Spanish, was slowing down a little. While continuing to provide José with direct instruction in English for at least one hour per day, the team had a bilingual aide work one-on-one with him on sight words and decoding reading skills in Spanish for two weeks. The aide used second-grade-level readers and stories to strengthen José's sound-symbol skills and basic reading skills. After two weeks of intervention at one hour per day, José's Spanish and English reading accuracy improved. The team then had the aide switch to an emphasis on comprehension of the content of the stories and readings. This one-on-one support continued with the aide accompanying José into the library to select books to read on his own and report back to her about them. The progress monitoring spreadsheet in his cumulative folder was expanded to include individual monitoring.

| Sociocultural Factors | ☑ | Selected Cross-Cultural Adaptation Risk Factors |
|---|---|---|
| Acculturation Level | ✓ | Recent immigrant, refugee, migrant, or resides on reservation |
| | | Does not interact much with majority culture peers or majority cultural group |
| | ✓ | Displays confusion in locus of control |
| | ✓ | Displays heightened stress or anxiety in cross-cultural interactions |
| | ✓ | Oral expression contains considerable code switching |
| | ✓ | Expresses or displays sense of isolation or alienation in cross-cultural interactions |
| % Checked: 83% | 5 | Out of 6 Total |

*(Continued)*

**Figure 20** (Continued)

| Sociocultural Factors | ☑ | Selected Cross-Cultural Adaptation Risk Factors |
|---|---|---|
| Cognitive Learning Style<br><br><br><br><br>% Checked: 83% | | Few cognitive learning strategies appropriate to classroom or school |
| | ✓ | Cognitive learning style different or inappropriate in relation to teacher's instructional style |
| | ✓ | Easily frustrated or low perseverance in completing tasks |
| | ✓ | Retains learning strategies that are no longer appropriate |
| | ✓ | Displays difficulty with task analysis |
| | ✓ | Displays difficulty with understanding and applying cause and effect |
| | 5 | Out of 6 Total |
| Culture & Language<br><br><br><br><br><br>% Checked: 50% | ✓ | Comes from non-English speaking home |
| | ✓ | Comes from a culture or ethnic group different from mainstream America |
| | ✓ | Family emphasizes support of family or community/group over individual effort |
| | | Comes from non-English speaking geographic area |
| | | Has culturally appropriate behaviors that are different from expectations of mainstream |
| | | There is no support in the home for bilingual and bicultural development. |
| | 3 | Out of 6 Total |
| Experiential Background<br><br><br><br><br><br><br><br>% Checked: 11% | | High family mobility |
| | | Limited or sporadic school attendance |
| | ✓ | Low socioeconomic status |
| | | Little exposure to subject or content or not familiar with material |
| | | Disrupted early childhood development |
| | | Few readiness skills |
| | | Does not know how to behave in classroom |
| | | Different terms/concepts for subject areas or materials and content |
| | | Uses survival strategies that are not appropriate in the classroom |
| | 1 | Out of 9 Total |
| Sociolinguistic Development<br><br><br><br><br><br><br>% Checked: 38% | | Does not speak English |
| | ✓ | Limited academic language in native language |
| | | Limited social language in English |
| | | Rarely speaks in class |
| | | Speaks only to cultural peers |
| | ✓ | Limited academic language in English |
| | ✓ | Asks a peer for assistance in understanding |
| | | Appears to know English but cannot follow English directions in class |
| | 3 | Out of 8 Total |

**Figure 20** Excerpt From Sociocultural Need Checklist for José after 20 Months

# Resolution or Referral 5

## PRISIM Step 5. Resolution or Referral

*Reviewing and analyzing the information gathered during the progress monitoring part of the problem-solving process to determine if the student requires additional screening and assessment (formal referral) or if sufficient progress has been documented to take the student out of the intensive individualized intervention and place him or her back in less intensive instructional settings similar to Step 2 or Step 3 settings. In programs using the tiered RTI or RTII model, this step coincides with the decision to stop Tier 3 interventions and move on to Tier 4. The intervention team reviews all instruction and intervention up to this point and makes data-based decisions on whether to continue intensive individualized interventions, to return the student to a less intensive group intervention setting, or to begin a formal evaluation and assessment procedure.*

Berkeley, Bender, Peaster, and Sanders (2009) stated that in all three-tier models, special education placement is considered a separate process that occurs after RTI/RTII remediation interventions have been exhausted. However, they note inconsistencies regarding when the special education referral process can be initiated.

Most programs for CLD students with learning and behavior problems involve some type of staged, pre-referral, or tiered intervention, and typically, special education services are only considered after students have progressed through Tier 3 (though some programs begin to conduct special education referrals after Tier 2). Within the PRISIM process, we recommend that CLD students be referred for a full individual evaluation (FIE) at any point that it is determined and documented that their learning and behavior

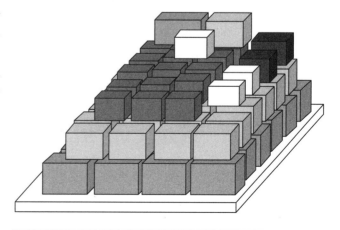

**Figure 21** Implementing strategies from different layers across the levels of the PRISIM pyramid

problems are not due to cultural or linguistic differences and are beyond the capacity of general education and language and cultural support personnel. Referrals to an FIE are appropriate for CLD students when verifiable documentation exists that shows that the student's limited English proficiency is not the most significant contributing factor in his or her learning or behavior problem. Culture, acculturation level, and language acquisition may contribute to the learning and behavior problems, but to justify a referral to an FIE, documentation must show that they are not determining factors for the learning and behavior problem. Other factors that validate the need for an FIE of a CLD student include:

- Poor communicative proficiency in the home as compared to siblings and age peers in bilingual environments, especially when this lack is noticed by the parents
- English language development that appears to be significantly different than that of peers who are also learning English as a second language
- Noted developmental delays or other at-risk conditions

Referral to FIE is a crucial element of the problem-solving and assessment process because misinterpretation of referral data may have considerably adverse effects on students, especially those from different cultural backgrounds (Stefanakis, 1998). A referral to FIE indicates the need for more complete and comprehensive assessment, based in part on the fact that insufficient progress has been made as a result of intensive interventions within the RTI or RTII process. In their study, however, Ysseldyke and Algozzine (1982) found that the decision to place a student in special education was primarily based on the teachers' reasons for referral, even when the results of academic and behavioral assessment measures did not support those comments. The element of referral in the problem-solving process for CLD students is thus an extremely important area of concern. A teacher's referral of a CLD student for assistance or FIE indicates the need for more complete and comprehensive problem solving, based in part on the fact that insufficient progress was made as a result of RTI or RTII interventions. The initial task of the team who receives the referral to FIE is to determine whether a comprehensive evaluation is warranted, based on the information gathered during the RTI or RTII portion of the problem-solving process. At this point, cultural and linguistic factors should already have been considered and found to not be significant contributing factors to the student's learning and behavior problems. To facilitate this decision, a checklist is often helpful, but it should never take the place of a comprehensive review of all documents and screening.

## EXAMPLE REFERRAL CHECKLIST FOR CLD STUDENTS

- Document that the student received sufficient prior instruction
- Document that the student received sufficient and appropriate prior language acquisition assistance
- Document that acculturation and language issues were addressed during the RTI and RTII process in an adequate and sufficient manner
- Document that acculturation and language issues can be excluded as significant contributing factors in the student's problems

- Document that RTI or RTII was appropriate and sufficient to determine the CLD student's capacity to achieve when provided with specific cross-cultural and bilingual interventions where applicable
- Document that RTI or RTII was appropriate and sufficient to resolve the CLD student's presenting problems
- Document that the CLD student's response to intensive instructional intervention strategies was inappropriate, inadequate, unresolvable, or otherwise troubling
- List unanswered questions

At the time of referral to FIE, the team should ensure that all pertinent information gathered during RTI or RTII instruction, as well as intervention activities, is compiled and available to the team responsible for the FIE. Personnel making the referral to FIE will facilitate the process by succinctly and objectively outlining on the referral form the suspected problem and the information obtained during the problem-solving, RTI and RTII stage. It is important to remember that the reason for referral to FIE may be a significant contributing factor in potential placement decisions; the person or team making the referral must ensure that the referral is accurate and relevant in the context of the CLD student's situation. This includes ensuring that socio-cultural factors (level of acculturation, rate of acculturation, language acquisition, socioeconomic status, and other factors) have been considered and, though part of the CLD student's learning and behavior profile, have not been found to be significantly contributing factors to the student's problems. In essence, one purpose of problem-solving activities is to gather sufficient information to ascertain the role of sociocultural factors in the exhibited learning and behavior problems. If the referral portion of the problem-solving process is completed appropriately and a referral to FIE is made, the following items will be evident:

1. Sociocultural information that has been compiled suggests whether acculturation, culture, and language factors are primary contributors to the student's learning or behavior problem or that other factors contribute significantly to the suspected learning and behavior problem.

2. Specific attempts to remedy the problems through the use of appropriate differentiated instruction and strategic interventions were documented and insufficient progress was made.

3. All information, instruction, interventions, and screening data were monitored regularly and over specific problem-solving periods of time.

4. All data compiled from the progress monitoring during problem-solving sessions were documented accurately and organized prior to an FIE.

5. Data compiled during problem-solving sessions were used to guide assessment procedures used in the FIE.

6. The decision was made that the CLD student's learning and behavior problems were more complex than could be addressed through general education, including differentiated support and ELL services.

7. A comprehensive FIE is necessary to determine more complete and appropriate forms of remediation.

The next stage of the assessment process, evaluation and staffing, begins on completion of the problem-solving stage, though problem solving with progress monitoring may certainly continue as part of the general monitoring of the CLD student's achievement on an IEP, should that be determined to assist the student's success. This is only possible when a culturally and linguistically diverse student has an unresolved learning or behavior problem that needs more than the instruction and intervention provided within the regular program. A district must address the following elements to conclude that referral to FIE is warranted:

1. A specific point in the intervention process has been identified for making a final decision to refer or not refer for an FIE.

2. An identified and trained team is responsible for making the decision to refer to FIE based on documented and monitored interventions of increasing intensity and of sufficient duration.

3. Documentation is adequate and appropriate to terminate the tiers of intensive intervention and move to a referral.

4. Documentation is used to certify that the learning or behavior problem is not due to the student's cultural or linguistic difference or to his or her level of acculturation.

5. Documentation exists to identify the student's language and acculturation needs in addition to any unresolved learning or behavior problems.

6. There is a process for documenting the results of the tiered intervention periods and how these were used to justify the referral to FIE.

After a referral to FIE, a comprehensive evaluation is scheduled and relevant specialists test and assess the student. The specialists' tasks are to reach a data-based decision regarding the best service or combination of services for this student and to determine if the student meets the eligibility requirements for special education services. If the specialists determine that the student is eligible, they will recommend a targeted services plan or an IEP that includes a plan for monitoring.

Educators want information that relates to the classroom learning environment, to students' learning and behavior problems within that environment, and to particular circumstances in which students can perform learning tasks successfully. Knowing when, how, and in what way a student can do something helps in planning for success, effective teaching, and optimal learning. Educators are also concerned with the collection of information related to students' socioeconomic background, home environment, and other out-of-school experiences. Including qualified bilingual and culturally and linguistically knowledgeable personnel on the problem solving and evaluation team is one way to address this. Providing consistent and regular training about the diverse populations that exist within the school enrollment area is another. The team conducting the FIE is constrained by federal regulations that do not apply during the problem solving and progress monitoring process per se. These include the need for signed approval forms, the required presence of parents, specific guidelines about providing interpreters for parents and translation of materials, and specific timelines for completion of the process. As a result of these concerns, the team usually involves members whose primary function is to determine an appropriate special education placement, but it may not include education professionals who know much about the culture, language, and acculturation of CLD students and what constitutes a least restrictive environment for such learners when they also have a disabling condition. Such teams must address the special needs of culturally and linguistically different students who also have disabilities; therefore, they should be composed of educators who can respond to those special needs. The team is only as effective as the skills and competencies of its members, and individuals involved in the instruction and assessment of diverse students should possess several competencies to ensure the attainment of the most meaningful and accurate information. Baca and Cervantes (2003) discussed the type of skills needed by team members involved in the assessment and instruction of CLD students with disabilities or CLDE students (culturally and linguistically diverse exceptional students). In addition to the usual range of abilities in assessment and instruction, one or more members of the team must also possess the following skills:

1. Knowledge of the appropriate use of instruments and procedures to assess language proficiency and first and second language abilities

2. Knowledge of the principles utilized to select a measure designed for use with students from the target populations, including but not limited to consideration of reliability, validity, norms, standards for administration, interpretation of outcomes, and sources of cultural bias

3. Knowledge of limitations of language assessment that result from examiner role, testing situation, content selection, questioning, dialect varieties of the target language, use of interpretation, and social-emotional factors

4. Ability to apply the information from testing, observations, and parent and teacher interviews to identify (a) baseline levels of skills and comprehension, (b) conditions under which skill acquisition can occur most efficiently, (c) the sequence of instructional activities needed, and (d) a plan for evaluation of both process and performance objectives

5. Knowledge and application of appropriate collaboration skills related to working with educational staff and parents in planning and implementing IEPs for diverse pupils demonstrating exceptionality

6. Ability to devise or adapt existing instruments for assessing diverse pupils, which may include developing (a) new normative data appropriate to the population and (b) informal instruments appropriate to the population

7. Knowledge of factors that influence second language acquisition, including use, motivation, attitude, personality, cognition, and the first language

8. Knowledge of the cognitive and language development of a normally developing CLD and CLDE student

9. Knowledge of cultural factors, including semantic and pragmatic systems, as they relate to sociolinguistic environment (i.e., parent-student, school-student interaction)

10. Knowledge of the dynamics of the interpretation procedure, including but not limited to the establishment of rapport with participants; kinds of information loss inherent in the interpretation procedure (such as omissions, additions, and substitutions); the use of appropriate nonverbal communication, methods, and techniques of interpretation and translation; the importance of obtaining accurate translations; the need to procure translations that do not reflect personal evaluations of the person whose remarks are being interpreted; and efforts to minimize the interpreter's elaborated responses or questions

11. Ability to plan and execute pre- and postassessment conferences, including in cross-cultural bilingual settings

An additional competency related to Item 10, on the preceding list, is the ability of the team to decide whether the services of an interpreter are necessary. An interpreter can translate the test or other assessment techniques, prepare the student and parents for the assessment process, interpret student responses, and facilitate communication with the parents during meetings. An interpreter may be necessary when a bilingual professional is not available, when it is inappropriate to have a peer or sibling translate, when the student is not literate in his or her dominant language, or when no tests are available in the student's dominant language. It is important to remember that the ability to speak a language well and the ability to translate are two distinct skills and are not necessarily found in all bilingual persons. The reauthorized IDEA has specific guidelines about providing interpreters for limited English proficient parents during IEP meetings and when a CLD student is being considered for placement in special education.

Among the skills needed by professionals who utilize the services of interpreters is the ability to plan and execute pre- and postdiagnostic conferences with the interpreter. In these conferences, the school professional trains and orients the interpreter to the purposes and procedures appropriate to formal testing, interviews, observations, and other assessment activities. Perhaps one of the most important skills the school professional needs is the ability to work with the interpreter, which entails ensuring trust between the person conducting the assessment and the interpreter, knowing how to record the behavior of the interpreter in testing situations, and being able to effectively convey information to the interpreter so an accurate translation can be facilitated. Professionals may need preparation to work effectively with interpreters, and the training of interpreters is an ongoing process that takes into account the current activities of the school assessment personnel.

The CLD student is assessed, as are all referred students, in all areas related to the suspected disability, including, when appropriate, health, vision, hearing, social and emotional status, general intelligence, academic performance, vocational skills, communicative status, and motor abilities. The process for a CLD student who is also LEP differs in that this assessment should occur in both the first and second language of the student and address his or her acculturation level. Thus, the composition of the team for particular CLD and CLDE students may vary.

All tests and screening materials must be evaluated prior to administration for cultural and linguistic bias. The results of the FIE are to be provided to the parents, or persons in parental relationships, in their most proficient language. The information gathered and evaluated will provide the basis of an individualized service plan or an IEP.

# TESTING

To ensure eligibility for and access to special programs, when appropriate, it is imperative that students be tested thoroughly. A combination of formal and informal assessment procedures should be used to determine the student's level of functioning and possible disability. Each school district must establish procedures to assure that testing and evaluation materials and procedures utilized for the purposes of evaluation and placement of disabled students are selected and administered so as not to be racially, linguistically, or culturally discriminatory. Such materials or procedures shall be provided and administered in the student's native language or mode of communication, as well as English, unless it is clearly not feasible. No single procedure shall be the sole criterion for determining an appropriate educational program for a student. The assessment of CLD students should take into consideration the following issues:

- Tests and evaluation materials must be provided and administered in the language or languages most likely to provide meaningful data regarding the performance objective of the assessment.
- Tests should be as culturally and linguistically nonbiased as possible, and items known to be problematic should be identified prior to administration.
- Tests and other assessment procedures should include those tailored to assess specific areas of educational need and not merely those that are designed to provide a general intelligence quotient (IQ).
- A structured observation of the CLD student in his or her primary educational setting and a home language observation should be conducted.

- Student's behavior throughout the testing situation should be recorded and analyzed.
- Persons who possess knowledge and skills related to both cultural and linguistic dimensions of diversity should administer all tests.

One way to adapt tests for culturally and linguistically diverse students is to evaluate the instruments for content and language bias. Bias occurs for many reasons: experiential background, socioeconomic status, family history, cultural and sociolinguistic background, gender, and other variables. Most general aptitude and ability tests rely on a student's previous experience and exposure to mainstream cultural concepts and, therefore, are of little educational use in assessing students from diverse cultural and linguistic backgrounds. The tasks included in the most frequently used standardized tests require a relatively high level of academic language in English. Therefore, the CLD student might be judged as having an ability deficit when, in reality, test performance merely exhibits differences in experiential background and limited English proficiency.

The first, and perhaps simplest, step in adaptation is to conduct a visual and structural overview of the illustrations in a test to determine if they are within the student's experiential background. It is also important to identify the standardization data to determine the representation of the normed population sample. This should be followed by an evaluation of the response modes that the testing instrument requires. If the assessment concern is whether or not the CLD student knows the multiplication facts or can recognize colors, the test must actually measure this ability and not the student's English proficiency in this area. Several nonverbal tools have been developed to assess general cognitive ability without relying on spoken directions in English or on gestures based on American educational patterns (Bracken & Naglieri, 2003).

The two most controversial issues in the assessment of CLD students are standardization and norming. According to Hammill (1987), standardization is applicable to all assessment techniques and knowledge of reliability. Tests that are highly standardized are considered formal assessments, while tests lacking standardization are considered informal assessments. Test validity is important when interpreting data collected from any assessment technique (e.g., analytic teaching, interviews, observations, testing). Hammill (1987) also noted that, while norms are often associated with standardized devices, their presence is by no means an essential element of standardization; in many cases norms are superfluous. With precise and consistent administrative procedures, testing and other assessment techniques adapted for use with culturally and linguistically diverse students can yield reliable, valid results and can be interpreted consistently without being norm-referenced.

For example, in many test constructions, items become increasingly difficult and the scoring and interpretation of such tests are a progression of item difficulty that was normed with a population that may not have included students of diverse linguistic and cultural backgrounds. Tests that use geometric patterns and no written language illustrate this inappropriateness. The patterns often become increasingly complicated and asymmetrical, and when a student misses several consecutive items, the examiner assumes a ceiling level has been reached and testing is discontinued. However, studies show that Crow students do better on the later portions of the test than on the beginning, "easier" portions.

Chesarek (1981) suggested that often performance is related to the cultural use of asymmetry, a concept that test designers and administrators need to bear in mind when assessing culturally and linguistically diverse learners.

Since it often takes ELL students five or more years to catch up academically in English, standardized achievement tests frequently underestimate an ELL student's academic progress and potential (O'Malley & Valdez-Pierce, 1996).

Although aware of the cultural and linguistic bias inherent in tests, most professionals see test scores as true measures of students' achievement and performance and often accept test scores as the sole basis for determining the instructional needs of students.

An additional component to testing CLD students is that the person who administers the test must be *functionally familiar* with the student's communication style and communicative repertoire. Functional familiarity goes beyond sensitivity to the standard, literate use of the native language. It requires that the test administrator senses how students can be helped to maximize their communication knowledge as they respond to test questions (Duran, 1994). This does not solely relate to ELL and LEP students, but also to students from minority cultures. Students' reactions and impressions are influenced by their home culture, which could lead students from other geographic locations or non-majority ethnic groups to respond in what could be considered an inappropriate way. The major underlying problem with formal assessment of CLD students for special education purposes is the lack of adequate connection between assessment outcomes and the subsequent instruction that is provided as a result of special education classification (Heller, Holtzman, & Messick, 1982).

It is important to remember that every test administered in English to a non-native English speaker becomes, in large part, a language test, and therefore, it may not in fact measure what it is intended to measure. Attention should be given to the assessment of the student's range of communicative competence in English across naturalistic settings, in addition to obtaining information about a student's problem-solving competencies in specific skill areas via an array of assessment instruments and devices. The following guidelines should be followed in the collection of the assessment data, as determined by the nature of the referral. All data should look at in which ways the student is and is not successful at various tasks.

## Observational Data

Observational data are needed in order to provide systematic and objective information regarding the student's behavior in formal and informal contexts by someone other than the referring person. Information should include the following: peer dynamics within the cultural group, amount of group participation when using the native language and when using English, classroom structure and organization, characteristics of the teaching/learning environment, and student-teacher interactions.

## Intellectual Assessment Data

Assessment of cognitive functioning should be conducted by a bilingual certified psychologist who is sensitive to the cultural background of the student and aware of indications of culturally appropriate behavior that may be demonstrated throughout the testing situation. Standardized intelligence tests must be valid. This means that if the normative population does not apply to the child, if the test items are culturally or linguistically inappropriate, or if the test must be modified during administration, then it is unethical to use standardized test scores to qualify that student to receive special education services.

Scores obtained from tests translated but not standardized on the student's cultural group or translated by the examiner during the assessment process may not be used as representative of the student's present performance. The information collected and reported should be of a descriptive nature. Reports should state the language in which the tests were administered and whether a translator or interpreter was used during the assessment.

## Adaptive Behavior Data

Adaptive behavior should be assessed within the linguistic and cultural framework of the student. When recording the adaptive behavior of language-minority pupils, one must include their learning styles, approaches to learning, communication strategies, psychomotor abilities, and aspirations. Much of the adaptive behavior information will be obtained from observing the student in different situations and in different settings. It may also be acquired from interviewing parents, siblings, peers, and significant others using a systematic, objective framework.

## Social/Emotional Behavior Data

Social/emotional behavior data should be collected through informal and formal means and should be objectively reported in terms of appropriate behavior within the linguistic and cultural framework of the family and community. Consideration should also be given to the student's level of acculturation and use of behavioral roles and rules associated with language and culture.

## Sociocultural Information

When collecting data on students from culturally diverse backgrounds, all aspects of the student's environment should be considered. Interviews and informal measures may be used to collect sociocultural information. This information should be documented by the bilingual social worker in relation to home and family responsibilities, cultural practices and behavior patterns, traditional versus nontraditional values, the role of education, and religious beliefs.

## Academic/Educational Test Data

As explained previously, standardized tests are valid only for those populations included in the standardization population of the test. If a test used to assess a CLD student is not valid for the student, informal assessment tools may be the best alternative. When informal assessment techniques are used, clinicians should describe the tasks presented, how they were presented, the child's responses, and the basis for the conclusions drawn from the behaviors described. As per the intellectual assessment, mentioned previously, scores obtained from tests that were translated but not standardized on the student's cultural group or translated by the examiner during the assessment processes may not be used as representative of the student's present performance. The information collected and reported should be of a descriptive nature. Reports should state the language(s) in which the tests were administered and whether a translator was used during the assessment. Again, if the normative population does not apply to the child, if the test items are culturally or linguistically inappropriate, or if the test must be modified during administration, then it is unethical to use standardized test scores to qualify that student to receive special education services.

## Language Assessment

The student's development in both the L1 and the L2 should be assessed, and current levels of proficiency in different skill areas (i.e., oral, writing, reading) should be established. Such language assessment should include data in language proficiency that is related to both social language (informal communication skills) and to academic language (formal communication skills) that is necessary for cognitive/academic environments. Language observations should include language in natural communication settings in various contexts, including the verbal and nonverbal strategies between the parent or guardian and the child.

The assessment of language development should include the following components, in both the native language and in English: prelanguage requisites, receptive language abilities, expressive language abilities, communicative competence (pragmatics), functional language usage, and language used for academic tasks (reading, comprehension, oral dictation, the ability to retell a story, etc.). The student's proficiency in different contexts and in both the L1 and L2 should be documented (e.g., face to face communication, interpersonal communication, academic literacy).

Language and phonological assessment should take into consideration the differences between the sound and grammatical system of English and the student's other-than-English language(s). In assessing the student's abilities in his or her languages, the dialect or language employed by the native community should be used as the norm, with consideration given to phonetic, semantic, and syntactic variations within each dialect. Also important are the age of the student when the second language was introduced and the manner in which it was introduced.

The language assessment of the ELL/LEP student is crucial because language data is essential to distinguishing characteristics associated with the normal second language acquisition process and those associated with a specific language disorder. If a language disability or a disorder of voice, fluency, or articulation is suspected, it should be evidenced in the native language of the student. A comprehensive speech and language assessment in the native language is needed, and thus, a bilingual licensed or certified speech and language specialist should conduct this assessment.

# ADAPTATION OF ASSESSMENTS

The evaluation team must document any modifications it has made from the standard procedure to adjust for language and culture differences (e.g., the presence of an additional adult or child, the use of an interpreter, a translated version of the instrument or procedure, or changes in the process or setting). The Selection Taxonomy for English Language Learner Accommodations, STELLA, has been developed over the last few years and is in final form (Kopriva and others, 2002, 2005, 2006). STELLA is intended to be used with K-12 students to assign accommodations to the range of ELL students for use on large-scale academic assessments. The CrossCultural Adaptation of Standardized Tests (CCAST; Collier, 2004b) is an example of a form that documents the precise modifications in standardized tests that may have been made. It also provides a vehicle for comparing standardized and modified achievement scores. Other similar forms or procedures may be followed to document these modifications.

It is extremely important that all team members document the cultural and linguistic accommodations that have been made and the language context of the testing itself. This documentation must accompany all files and reports on the CLD student.

## Evaluation Interpretation

Eligibility for special education is determined by the evaluation team (ET). The team will review and take into consideration all available assessment data, including the results of the instructional intervention team actions. The team develops a summary analysis to show which assessment instruments were used, any modifications for language or acculturation level, the scores, and the results. Elements that must be included in the evaluation report are as follows:

1. Impact of sociocultural environment
2. Modifications to tests and evaluation procedures, including translations and interpreters
3. Impact of translations and interpreters
4. Use of nonverbal tests and comparison of those results to other assessed areas
5. Effect of examiner's cross-cultural and linguistic competence
6. Cross-validation of information for home setting

Through the information gained from the assessment data, the ET records issues that are pertinent to the student's level of functioning, including L1 and L2 information. If the disability adversely affects the student's educational performance and creates a need for special education services, the student is determined eligible and the ET members sign the report. This becomes the basis for the IEP.

Sometimes modifying the scoring and interpretation of test results for CLD students is beneficial to the evaluation process. This procedure includes reviewing the test before administration to identify possibly biased or questionable items, modifying the interpretation of student errors, rescoring potentially biased items, and comparing the results of alternative scoring. If the rescoring shows little difference in performance, further student assessment is needed to determine eligibility for placement in special education. However, the influence of sociocultural factors should not be ruled out. If the rescoring shows moderate difference in performance, the student may need further eligibility assessment and programming that will address language and acculturation needs. If the rescoring shows considerable difference in performance, the student may need language and acculturation assistance. However, possible handicapping conditions cannot be ruled out as a factor in learning and behavior problems. The team must consider all assessment results during the staffing meeting, including considerations of intervention information, evaluation of sociocultural indicators, and evaluation of specific learning and behavior problems.

## Use of Standardized Norm-Referenced Tests

The composition of the population used for norming a test is the major concern in using standardized norm-referenced tests when assessing diverse students. The test designer must decide which population will provide the norms for the varied sociocultural populations examined. If, for example, a test designer's decision about establishing norms causes the test scores of one sociocultural group to be consistently higher or lower than those of another sociocultural group, the norm-referenced test may be biased against the group obtaining consistently lower test scores. When norm-referenced instruments are based on experiences that are unfamiliar to students from a certain sociocultural group, the rights of those students must be protected.

The *Larry P. v. Wilson Riles* case of 1979 exemplifies the concern about the use of standardized norm-referenced tests in the assessment of diverse students. The case, begun in 1970, was a class action suit against the San Francisco Unified School District and the California State Department of Education on behalf of African American students who were allegedly misclassified as educable mentally retarded based on invalid IQ test results. The case challenged the construct validity of standardized IQ tests as a measure of the learning potential of diverse students. As a result of the *Larry P.* case, California banned the use of standardized IQ tests for the assessment of diverse students for special education purposes.

The implications of this case extend far beyond testing for special education. Any use of an IQ test is prohibited if such assessment could lead to special education placement or services, even if the test is part of a comprehensive assessment plan. Since the case was based on bias inherent in standardization, norm-referenced interpretation, and content, it has far-reaching implications for the continued use of standardized norm-referenced tests with all culturally and linguistically diverse students.

To conclude this section, Step 5 in the PRISIM process is where data gathered during the progress monitoring part of the problem-solving process is reviewed and analyzed. After addressing the CLD student's learning and behavior issues at increasing levels of intensity, the diverse learner's presenting problems may be resolved or the RTI and RTII team may decide that more intensive efforts are considered necessary. If RTI and RTII efforts are unsuccessful in remediating or minimizing the potential learning or behavior problem, the team may make a formal referral for an in-depth evaluation to identify any undiagnosed learning and behavior problems or they may start another sequence of intensive individualized problem solving. In either situation, resolution or referral to further intervention, the strategies that have been shown to be effective in the learner's progress should become a regular part of the learning environment for the CLD or CLDE student. If access to bilingual materials resolves the student's comprehension difficulties, they should remain available to the student when he or she leaves the intensive individualized effort and returns to the usual large and small group instruction activities within the general classroom. In the vast majority of situations, increasingly intensive interventions for CLD students result in resolution of their learning and behavior problems (Baca & Cervantes, 2003) within eight to ten weeks. The intervention and monitoring process also results in information about what the student can and cannot do, which informs further evaluation should this be necessary.

# JOSÉ CASE STUDY

## Resolution or Further Intervention

Returning to our case study student, a review of the individual intensive interventions used at PRISIM 4 Tier 3 illustrates the team's next process decision. The team identified strategies to use in intervention and secondary strategies to implement if the first ones proved ineffective. An example of this planning design for progress monitoring is shown in Figure 22. All teaching staff went over task steps and scripts for consistent sequencing, and a bilingual aide worked one-on-one with José in the use of a self-monitoring checklist. José used advanced organizers in his writing and math lessons and preview and organization strategies in his math and social studies readings. A bilingual aide showed José how to use a math word problem solving strategy while the reading specialist pulled José out of the general classroom and reviewed basic sound-symbol relationships. The bilingual ESL teacher reviewed Spanish phonemes and highlighted similarities and differences between Spanish and English. José had access to Spanish content textbooks that supported his math, social studies, and science course work. José's Spanish and English reading accuracy and rate of reading improved, and his content area achievement showed steady progress. He also showed some improvement in reading comprehension in both languages.

| Target Concern | Intervention Selected | Intervention Modification | Duration | Outcomes of Intervention |
|---|---|---|---|---|
| Cognitive Learning | Sorting | Guided rehearsal | | |
| | Rehearsal | Visualization | | |
| Acculturation and Adaptation | Consequences | Model, demonstrate | | |
| | Self-monitoring | Demonstrate, shorten time | | |
| Literacy and Content Learning | Generalizing from descriptions | Demonstration, modeling | | |
| | Generating written sentences | Guided practice, demonstration | | |

**Figure 22** Designing Progress Monitoring

This intensive individualized intervention continued for seven weeks, with staff documenting José's responses on the comprehensive progress monitoring spreadsheet. An example of this spreadsheet is shown in Figure 23. The specific objectives and the individualized intensive interventions used in sequence to address these objectives are shown along with the performance goal line the team identified as appropriate for José. The goal line represents the average performance of José's peer group of CLD learners. The squiggly line represents José's performance in response to the various interventions that were implemented.

## PRISIM 5 Decision to Continue or Evaluate

As can be seen on the progress monitoring chart (Figure 23), José made progress in all areas of intervention. However, his performance was still not equal to his peer group. José demonstrated through his response during the intensive individualized intervention that he had the capacity to learn academic content in all areas and to become a successful reader in both English and Spanish. He showed that he could attend to tasks and complete them, and he exhibited an ability to increase self-control over his behavior. The team recognized that his response to intervention showed that there did not appear to be an undiagnosed disability, in the legal sense, that was impeding José's ability to succeed in school, but the team still worried about the achievement gap between him and his CLD peers and the fact that it took so much support and effort to bring his learning and behavior closer to that of his peers.

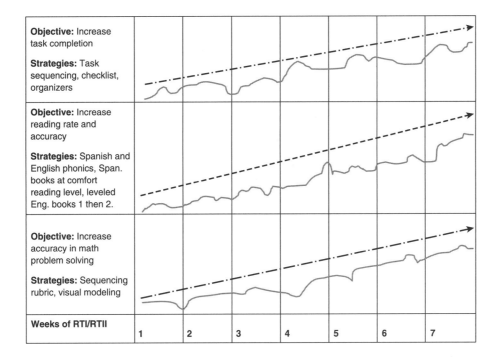

**Figure 23** José's Intervention Progress Monitoring

The team summarized everything they had done for José and his response to the interventions on a form similar to that shown in Table 6, and they asked for a meeting with the school psychologist, counselor, social worker, special education teacher, and principal to discuss further actions for José. An actual example of the instruction and intervention strategies implemented for José is shown in Figure 24.

**Table 6**   Example of José's Intervention Summary form

| Student: JOSÉ | DOB: | | Current Grade: |
|---|---|---|---|
| Language(s) student speaks other than English: Quechua, Spanish | | | |
| Language(s) parent/guardian speaks to student: Quechua | | | |
| Language(s) student speaks?<br>Quechua, Spanish, English | With parent/guardian?<br>Quechua | | With sibling(s)?<br>Quechua, English |
| With neighborhood friends?<br>Spanish | With school friends?<br>Spanish, English | | With others?<br>Spanish, English |
| Are parents aware of your concerns:  ☒   Yes        ☐   No | | | |

| **School Experience Outside United States or Canada** | | |
|---|---|---|
| Country(ies) *Peru* | Age started school *7yrs* | Number of interruptions |
| Circle each grade completed outside the United States/Canada | | |
| N   Pre   K   ①   ②   3   4   5   6   7   8   9   10   11   12 | | |

| **School Experience Inside United States or Canada** | | |
|---|---|---|
| Age started school  *9 yrs* | Number of interruptions | ☒ U.S.        ☐ Canada |
| Circle each grade completed inside the United States/Canada | | |
| N   Pre   K   1   2   ③   ④   5   6   7   8   9   10   11   12 | | |

| Days absent: *2* | |
|---|---|
| Number of schools attended *2* | Retained?   ☐ Yes   ☒ No      Grade(s) |

**Adaptation Concerns**

| Sociocultural Area | Order of Concern | Prior Instruction | Duration of Intervention | Outcomes of Intervention |
|---|---|---|---|---|
| Acculturation | 2 | | | |
| Cognitive learning | 1 | | | |
| Culture and language | | | | |
| Experiential background | | | | |
| Sociolinguistic development | 3 | | | |

| A. Achievement in English | 5 | 4 | 3 | 2 | 1 | Progress | | |
|---|---|---|---|---|---|---|---|---|
| 1. Receptive language, social comprehension | | | | x | | ☒ | yes | ☐ no |
| 2. Receptive language, academic comprehension | | | | x | | ☒ | yes | ☐ no |
| 3. Expressive language, social interaction | | | | x | | ☒ | yes | ☐ no |
| 4. Expressive language, academic interaction | | | | x | | ☒ | yes | ☐ no |
| 5. Reading | | | | x | | ☐ | yes | ☒ no |
| 6. Written language | | | | | x | ☐ | yes | ☒ no |
| 7. Mathematics | | | | x | | ☒ | yes | ☐ no |
| 8. Other: | | | | | | ☐ | yes | ☐ no |
| **B. School Behavior** | **5** | **4** | **3** | **2** | **1** | **Progress** | | |
| 1. Positive peer interactions | | | | x | | ☒ | yes | ☐ no |
| 2. Positive adult interactions | | | | | x | ☒ | yes | ☐ no |
| 3. Works independently | | | | | x | ☒ | yes | ☐ no |
| 4. Cooperates in a group | | | | x | | ☒ | yes | ☐ no |
| 5. Able to focus/attend | | | | | x | ☐ | yes | ☒ no |
| 6. Responsive | | | | x | | ☒ | yes | ☐ no |
| 7. Follows rules | | | | | x | ☐ | yes | ☒ no |
| 8. Other: | | | | | | ☐ | yes | ☐ no |

| Academic Interventions | Frequency | Duration | Progress |
|---|---|---|---|
| Active processing | Every day in content | 3 weeks | Increased accuracy and focus from baseline to 80% |
| Adapted instructional materials | | | |
| Cognitive learning strategies | 2 hours a day | 3 weeks | Increased processing and accuracy from baseline to 80% |
| Consulted resource people | | | |

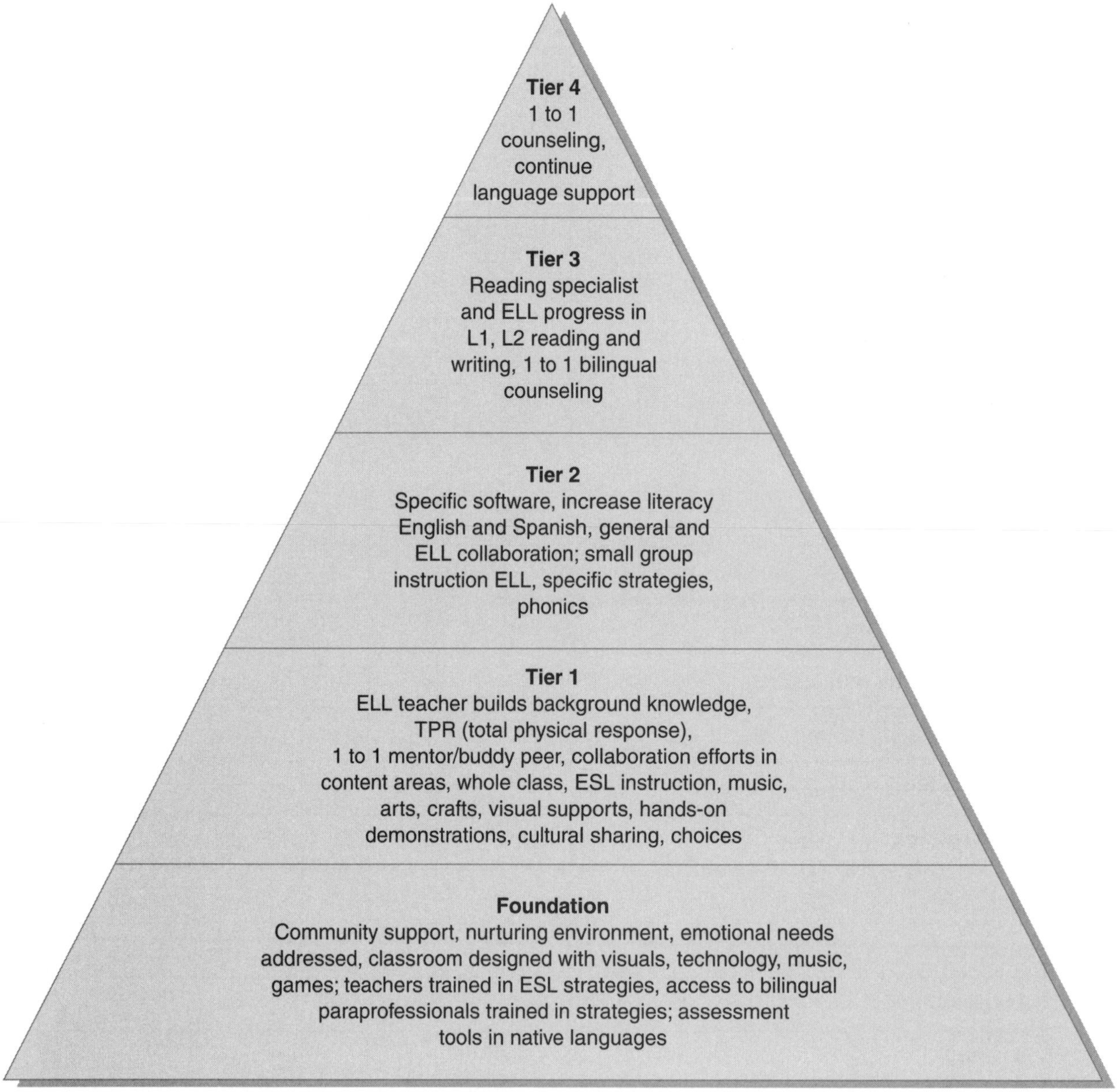

**Tier 4**
1 to 1 counseling, continue language support

**Tier 3**
Reading specialist and ELL progress in L1, L2 reading and writing, 1 to 1 bilingual counseling

**Tier 2**
Specific software, increase literacy English and Spanish, general and ELL collaboration; small group instruction ELL, specific strategies, phonics

**Tier 1**
ELL teacher builds background knowledge, TPR (total physical response), 1 to 1 mentor/buddy peer, collaboration efforts in content areas, whole class, ESL instruction, music, arts, crafts, visual supports, hands-on demonstrations, cultural sharing, choices

**Foundation**
Community support, nurturing environment, emotional needs addressed, classroom designed with visuals, technology, music, games; teachers trained in ESL strategies, access to bilingual paraprofessionals trained in strategies; assessment tools in native languages

**Figure 24** Example of Tiered Intervention Strategies for José

# Integrated Services 6

**PRISIM Step 6. Integrated Services and Cross-Cultural IEPs**

*Determining a student's individualized instructional needs and outlining a monitoring and service plan. If special education and related services are appropriate, the student is served in a program that meets the student's unique instructional needs and an individualized plan of instruction or individual educational plan (IEP) is developed. The IEP must include language and culture accommodations that reflect the interaction of the student's unique and special needs, as well as the student's specific language, acculturation, and culture needs. In programs using the tiered RTI or RTII model, this step is sometimes incorporated into Tier 4.*

Not all models consist of three tiers; some add a fourth tier. Often, the fourth tier is referral and placement in special education. Some four-tier models are similar to the three-tier, problem-solving model, with the fourth tier serving as the most intensive, extended, specially-designed, and individualized instruction. Some four-tier models are similar to three-tier standard protocol models, where the fourth tier is an IEP.

Berkeley, Bender, Peaster, and Sanders (2009) stated that in all three-tier models, special education placement is considered a separate process that occurs after RTI and RTII remediation interventions have been exhausted. However, they noted inconsistencies regarding when the special education referral process can be initiated. Although most programs consider special education after students have progressed through Tier 3, some conduct special education referrals after Tier 2, and others allow special education referrals to be made at any point in the RTI and RTII process.

In the PRISIM problem solving model, CLD students can be referred for intervention within special education at any point that it is determined that their learning and behavior problems are not due to cultural or linguistic differences and effective learning cannot be sustained within general education (including CLD and ELL) instruction alone. The specially designed individualized instruction available within special education is a focused element of problem solving that addresses the unique learning and behavior needs of eligible CLDE students. Success is achieved when diverse learners are able to participate effectively at or near peers in all programs and content areas and sustain learning within a differentiated program.

After completing the full individual evaluation (FIE) and collecting all relevant data on the student they are examining, the team members hold a staffing meeting. During the staffing meeting, the team discusses the results of the evaluations and determines whether the CLD student is eligible for special education services. Three hypotheses are tested during the meeting: (1) The student's learning and behavior problems are primarily due to linguistic or sociocultural factors, (2) the student's problems are primarily due to a disabling condition, or (3) the student's problems are primarily due to a combination of linguistic, sociocultural factors and a disabling condition. Under current IDEA guidelines, if the first hypothesis is found to be true, the CLD student is not eligible for special education services. If the second or third hypothesis is found to be true, the team must prepare an IEP that accommodates the CLDE student's linguistic and sociocultural needs while addressing his or her special education needs.

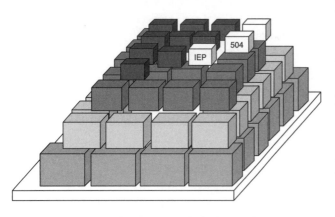

**Figure 25**   Adding a Layer of Specially Designed Instruction and Individualized Strategies to the PRISIM Pyramid

Finding the CLD student not eligible for special education services does not obviate the school staff from addressing how individual learning and behavior needs will be met within the context of the general and ELL instructional program.

The team must share and discuss the findings of evaluations of the student, the results of the intensive instructional interventions implemented with the student, the accumulated referral information, and any other information pertinent to each hypothesis. Analyzing hypotheses leads to service design decisions. For example, looking at the CLDE student's level and rate of acculturation throughout the time he or she has been in the district may show that the student's rate of acculturation and adaptation is normal and thus not a contributing factor in his or her presenting problem.

A diverse student who is referred for an FIE for unresolved learning or behavior problems must be assured of equitable process and decision making. The district must be able to account for specific concerns within the evaluation process:

1.  Specific cross-culturally competent personnel have participated in the process

2.  A sufficiently diverse team of professionals is used to assure equity and accuracy of assessment and interpretation

3.  There is a process and documentation that assures the planning and interpretation is appropriate for this CLDE student

4. Documentation is present to establish the presence of an identified disability

5. Documentation is present to establish that the CLDE student's learning and behavior problems are not principally due to the student's cultural or linguistic difference, level of acculturation, limited English proficiency, or access to adequate and appropriate prior instruction

6. Documentation is present to identify the CLDE student's continuing language and acculturation needs that must be addressed in addition to his or her identified disability

7. There is a process and documentation that assures the individualized learning plan addresses the CLDE student's language and acculturation needs, including language of instruction and services, in the context of interventions for specific disabilities

# DECISION

If the team finds that the diverse student's learning and behavior problems are due primarily to cultural or linguistic difference, level of acculturation, limited English proficiency, or access to adequate and appropriate prior instruction, the decision may be to return the student to the general education program with recommendations for addressing these needs. This necessitates consideration of returning to a Tier 1, Tier 2, or Tier 3 level of intensity as well as identifying specific intervention strategies that will remain part of the CLD student's instructional plan. In the dynamic PRISIM model, blocks of strategies and interventions that have proven effective for the individual CLD student's success accompany the student within any tier of instructional intervention.

If the team decides that the diverse student's learning and behavior problems are not primarily due to cultural or linguistic difference, level of acculturation, limited English proficiency, or access to adequate and appropriate prior instruction, it may identify the nature of the student's specific learning and behavior problems and recommend specific special education or related services. The team may also recommend specific special education services if it determines that the diverse student's problems are due to the presence of a disabling condition with the addition of a combination of cultural or linguistic difference, level of acculturation, or limited English proficiency. In the latter two cases, the team will develop an individualized plan of learning that addresses all of the diverse student's special needs, including those that are due to cultural or linguistic difference, level of acculturation, or limited English proficiency.

## Development of an Individualized Learning Plan for CLDE Students

The individualized learning, or educational, plan is usually based on a determination of the student's strengths and weaknesses in the areas of achievement, aptitude or ability, and emotional or behavioral competence. In addition to identifying the CLDE student's general competence in these areas, the individualized plan specifies instructional objectives and a sequence of actions for achieving these objectives through modification of instructional content, strategies, and setting. For CLDE students, these actions involve preparing a cross-culturally inclusive service plan, including appropriate language and acculturation interventions in all education settings, monitoring effectiveness, and matching needs and curricular elements.

The IEP and specially designed instructional plan, developed in consultation with all concerned parties, must be a comprehensive presentation of the CLDE student's total learning needs. This includes instructional guidelines and objectives to address the student's acculturation and language acquisition needs, as well as his or her unique special educational needs. In addition, it should address the integration of these services, indicating *who* is responsible for providing and maintaining culturally and linguistically appropriate instructional interventions as well as the context in with these CLD services will be sustained. Assistance by all personnel in implementing language and acculturation interventions is required. The IEP should also address *how* culturally and linguistically appropriate specially designed instructional interventions will be utilized in meeting the student's special needs. The steps involved in the development of an individualized plan for diverse students with special needs include the development of objectives related to the following:

- Home language development
- English or school language acquisition
- The facilitation of acculturation
- Academic achievement accommodations for his or her specific disabling condition
- The integration of specific culture and language interventions that address special education needs
- Identification of service providers responsible for implementing and monitoring the integration of these services in a comprehensive manner
- Time limits and specific, scheduled reevaluation formats, dates, and meetings
- Specific strategies for including CLDE students and families, including access to interpreters and translation of materials

The parents of the CLDE student participate in the planning of the individualized learning plan and must be included in IEP meetings. A notice for the IEP meeting must be provided to the parents in their most proficient language, and under current IDEA guidelines, if the native language or other mode of communication of the parent is not a written language, the district must take steps to ensure that

1. The notice is translated orally or by other means to the parent in his or her native language or other mode of communication

2. The parent understands the content of the notice

3. There is written evidence that these two requirements have been met

If the parents cannot attend the meeting, other methods need to be used to ensure parent participation, such as individual or conference calls with the parents or legal guardians of the student in their native language. The IEP meeting for each newly identified CLDE pupil shall be conducted as *soon* as possible, but no later than thirty days after the student's evaluation is completed. Participants in the IEP meetings for CLDE students should include each the following:

- Representative of the school district or other public agency
- Person knowledgeable about the language and acculturation needs of the student
- Student's special education teacher or therapist
- General education teachers in whose class the student is enrolled
- Parents or legal guardians
- Person knowledgeable about the evaluation procedures
- Person knowledgeable about all of the special education, ELL, and other service options
- Other individuals at the discretion of the district or other public agency

The student may be included in this meeting depending upon age, maturity, and level of understanding. Interpretation of the IEP must be provided in the parents' or guardians' native language, and the assessment report should be orally translated into their native language. If the parents or guardians of the CLDE student are literate in the home language, a translation of the IEP and assessment report may be provided. The preparation of the IEP document includes five steps: (1) review analysis and findings; (2) list CLDE student's needs; (3) identify appropriate cross-cultural interventions, approaches, and services; (4) identify timeline and expectations; and (5) identify monitoring schedule.

1. **Review:** The IEP meeting participants begin with a review of the documentation provided by the instructional intervention team and the evaluation, being especially attentive to the second language acquisition and acculturation needs of the CLDE student in relation to his or her special learning and behavior needs. The group develops a statement that describes the student's present level of performance in all areas under discussion. This includes a statement of the CLDE student's present level of acculturation, including his or her present levels of performance in the native language and in English. This statement of present levels of performance is written in the first portion of the IEP and forms the basis for identifying all of the student's needs.

2. **Needs:** The group next identifies specific needs that can be addressed with the services available within the school, the district, and the community. Among these will be a determination of the language of instruction within each area of concern. There may be some areas of concern where the native language of the student is more appropriate and some areas where English is more appropriate, depending upon the CLDE student's social and academic levels in both languages and his or

her present level of acculturation. The language of instruction in each area should be recorded on the IEP form. The group develops specific short- and long-term goals and objectives for each identified need. There should also be goals and objectives for facilitating the CLDE student's acculturation to the school system. The group also identifies appropriate objective criteria and evaluation procedures consistent with the student's linguistic abilities in the first and second language to measure all desired outcomes.

3. **Intervention:** The cross-cultural IEP group uses the list of goals and objectives to identify individual cross-cultural instructional interventions, strategies, and procedures for addressing each specific identified need. It also identifies the personnel who will be responsible for implementing these approaches. The group identifies desired proficiency outcomes for appropriate second language acquisition and acculturation interventions and which service providers will be responsible. Documentation is required when referrals to external services are needed. The IEP group generates a statement of the specific special education and related services to be provided. For the CLDE student, this description of special education and related services is summarized as follows:

   o The recommended program and level of bilingual special education services to be provided
   o Alternative testing procedures or modifications related to both limited English proficiency and disabling conditions
   o Specification of services to meet the linguistic and cultural needs of the CLDE student
   o The language(s) in which all services will be provided
   o Degree of participation with English-speaking children
   o Specification of language intervention in the native and second language (development, enrichment, remediation)
   o The facilitation of acculturation
   o Special education needs
   o Integration of specific culture and language interventions that address special education needs
   o The extent of instruction in subject or cognitive areas in the native language or in English, as appropriate
   o Identification of service providers responsible for implementing and monitoring the integration of these services
   o Identification of the extent to which the student will be involved in learning support (e.g., Bilingual/ESL, Migrant Education, and other support or related services)
   o Intensive instruction in ESL
   o Instruction that focuses on the student's abilities (linguistic and cognitive) while targeting the area of disability
   o The extent to which the student will participate with nondisabled (both CLD as well as English proficient) students in an integrated or inclusive setting
   o An explanation of the basis for rejecting specific indicated services

4. **Timeline:** After identifying appropriate instructional services, strategies, and approaches, the IEP group determines realistic timelines for each specific intervention and when and how the outcomes will be measured. This measurement must be described within the context of the CLDE student's second language acquisition and acculturation needs. The timeline includes the projected date for the initiation of special education and related services, the amount of time per day the pupil will receive such services, and whether the pupil is eligible for a twelve-month educational program. The timeline establishes the time limits for specific interventions and service options, as well as documenting the schedule for specific reevaluations and monitoring meetings.

5. **Monitoring:** Monitoring is the final component of the placement stage, and it completes the total assessment process for diverse students. Finally, the IEP group determines and includes an appropriate schedule for monitoring and retesting or reevaluating the CLDE student's progress with learning and behavior development. This schedule should include expected benchmarks for second language acquisition and acculturation for this culturally and linguistically diverse exceptional student. The IEP group identifies specific instruments and procedures that will be used and records these on their IEP form.

This assessment monitoring is a cyclical process. As prescribed services and interventions are implemented, the service providers are keeping note of and documenting the CLDE student's progress and responses to specific approaches and strategies. The plan for monitoring should indicate the individual responsible for each element of the monitoring process and should include (1) regular assessment and evaluation of the student's level of performance in targeted learning and behavior areas of concern; (2) regular assessment of the CLDE student's second language acquisition; (3) periodic review of his or her degree of acculturation and response to acculturative stress; and (4) monitoring the student's changing response to the school environment and to the acquisition of new cognitive-learning strategies.

Depending on the CLDE student's response to sociocultural prescriptions and interventions and to those prescribed to address the student's learning and behavior problem, the monitoring process may result in reassessing the placement decision and the student's return to the general education program. On the other hand, as the CLDE student successfully resolves the identified learning and behavior problems, additional problems may manifest. In addition, the CLDE student may continue to need assistance with second language acquisition and acculturation. If it is determined that the CLDE student has achieved the goals on his or her present IEP, but new needs have become manifest, monitoring should result in a reassessment of the student's needs and a subsequent revision of the IEP. The monitoring schedule includes annual and triennial reviews.

## Annual Reviews

At a reasonable time prior to conducting the annual review, notification is sent to the parents in their native language. All annual review proceedings must be understandable to the parents. For all CLDE students receiving special education services, the service provider must attend the conference. If the attendance of a bilingual professional is not possible, an interpreter must attend the meeting. The participation of bilingual professionals, interpreters, and translators must be documented in the IEP. At the annual review, the IEP of each CLDE student with disabilities must be reviewed. Information that should be available for this review includes the following:

1. Updated language proficiency test results in the native language and in English. This should include both social and academic language skills.

2. Updated acculturation level records (e.g., AQS results).

3. Current levels of performance as measured in accordance with the student's level of first and second language proficiency.

4. A statement concerning the language of instruction that is being used for each IEP goal and objective.

Implementation of any recommendations subsequent to the annual review should occur within 10 calendar days following the final recommendation, or as specified on the IEP. This may include those instances where there has been a change in the services provided from bilingual to monolingual or monolingual to bilingual.

## Triennial Evaluation

The triennial evaluation is a comprehensive reevaluation of a CLDE student with a disabling condition that is conducted every three years. Some districts review these placements every year or every two years. The same guidelines to determine if a bilingual assessment is needed apply to these evaluations. The purpose of the triennial evaluation for the CLDE student is the same as for monolingual students: to update the CLDE student's present levels of educational performance (including performance in both languages) and to analyze and document the CLDE student's instructional needs.

The placement process for CLDE students has two basic elements: (1) the placement of a diverse learner in special education for his or her unresolved learning or behavior problem, or (2) the return of the diverse learner to the regular instructional program. In both placement circumstances, the diverse learner may have language, culture, and acculturation needs that must continue to be addressed. School districts must attend to specific issues in both the placement and nonplacement elements in the placement process.

1. Personnel participating in the IEP are cross-culturally competent.

2. There is documentation and a process in place to assure the service plan is comprehensive and cross-culturally inclusive.

3. There is a process to identify appropriate language and acculturation interventions for the student in both the special and regular education setting.

4. There is a plan for monitoring the effectiveness of the language and acculturation interventions in the special education setting, as well as in the regular program.

5. There is a process to match the student's cross-cultural instructional needs with appropriate curricular elements.

6. Resource personnel are identified and available to assist educators in implementing language and acculturation interventions.

## BIAS IN SERVICE PLANS

According to Ysseldyke and Algozzine (1982), bias concerns are related to the manner in which our society evaluates the worth of an individual. The authors further stated that CLD students have traditionally been overrepresented in special education classes and that this occurrence has not changed in recent years. Although much concern has arisen over the collection of data in a nondiscriminatory manner, they stated that "the more immediate problems are biases in the decision-making process and abuse in the use of assessment data on which important decisions regarding students are made" (p. 135). Thus, the misuse or misinterpretation of assessment data may have significantly adverse effects on children, especially children from different cultures.

Figure 26 illustrates the sociocultural levels of development from Figure 9 with some of the most frequent special education placement categories mistaken for these cultural areas.

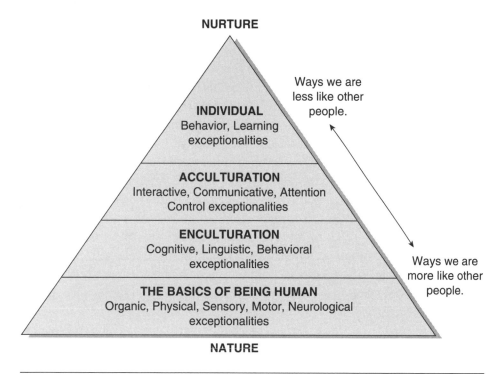

**Figure 26** Special Education Juxtaposed With Cultural Issues

A 2000 study, conducted by the Research on Learning Disabilities Center at the University of Minnesota, investigated the extent to which different kinds of assessment data were used in special education placement decisions. The 159 educators and school psychologists who participated in the study were asked to read a case-folder description of a child and provide a diagnostic decision concerning special education placement, and their decision-making behaviors concerning the placement were analyzed. According to the results, the reason for referral given by the referring teacher had a significant impact that biased service delivery and placement decisions. Also, those children who were referred for behavioral problems were significantly more often diagnosed and labeled as emotionally disabled than children referred for academic problems.

## EMOTIONAL AND BEHAVIORAL DISORDERS

According to Stephens, Blackhurst, and Magliocca (1982), the regular class teacher is often the first person to refer a child for behavioral problems. In reference to children from different cultures, Gonzales (1982) documented that it is important to know the child's capabilities in his or her own culture, as well as in the dominant culture. Stephens et al. (1982) added that the assessment of a child's behavior and learning must be completed in a variety of settings. Thus, the assessment of a culturally different child's suspected behavior and learning problems should occur in relation to the dominant culture, as well as the child's own culture.

According to the 2000 US Census, there remains considerable disproportionality in emotional and behavioral placements in public schools (Samuels, 2007). While proportionately the same percentage of mainstream students (*white* on the 2000 US Census) were identified and received services as being seriously emotionally disordered, a greater percentage of African American students were identified and placed in programs for the emotionally disordered than exist in the general population. This was also true of American Indian students. The disproportionality remains when controlling for differences in educational status, access to prenatal care, and poverty.

Assessment data may be misused or misinterpreted, specifically as it relates to culturally different children. Due to this, there is a need to assist regular classroom teachers, as well as other educators, in understanding the exhibited behaviors for which a culturally different child may be referred and the importance and relevancy of those referred behaviors in the child's own culture. Information concerning selected behaviors of culturally different children prior to the actual referral may assist in reducing some bias within the referral and decision-making process related to a culturally different child's need for special education placement.

A list of behaviors often exhibited by children with emotional or behavioral disorders (EBD) was investigated in relation to various CLD cultures, and the results are presented in Table 7.

**Table 7**  Sociocultural Factors Related to Emotional or Behavioral Disorders (EBD) Placements

| General Area | Selected Indication Behaviors | Sociocultural Considerations |
|---|---|---|
| Withdrawn behavior: | Does not respond when spoken to. Fails to talk, although has skill. Prefers to be alone. | Normal stage in second language acquisition and acculturation. Culturally appropriate to native culture. |
| Defensive behavior: | Loses belongings. Exhibits "I don't care" attitude. Demonstrates lack of responsibility. Wastes time. Arrives late. Cheats. Blames others. Shows difficulty in changing activities. | Presupposes familiarity with having belongings. Acculturation may cause anxiety and resistance to change. Concepts of time vary considerably from culture to culture. External locus of control may be taught or encouraged in some cultures. External vs. internal locus of control confusion results from acculturation process. Concepts of cheating/stealing vary from culture to culture. |
| Disorganized behavior: | Confuses time. Demonstrates poor living skills. Displays extreme social withdrawal. Has poor interpersonal relationships. | Concepts of time vary considerably from culture to culture. Culturally appropriate to native culture. Normal state in second language acquisition and acculturation. |
| Aggressive behavior: | Talks out in class. Fights or harasses others. Behaves impulsively. Talks back to teacher. Does not follow class rules. | Culturally appropriate in native culture. Presupposes familiarity with appropriate school behavior and language. |

As indicated, some research has shown the reason for referral to be a significant factor in the placement decision-making process. With reference to culturally different children, understanding how certain behaviors relate to different cultures is important if the child is to be appropriately referred and diagnosed for possible special education services.

## INTELLECTUAL EXCEPTIONALITIES

According to the 2000 US Census, disproportionality also exists in identification and services to students with mild to severe cognitive and intellectual disabilities (Samuels, 2007). Asian American and white students are disproportionately overrepresented in classes for the gifted and talented while

African American, Hispanic, and American Indian students remain underrepresented in these classes. This is also true for limited English proficient students, even those testing at very advanced levels on traditional IQ tests and other tests of cognitive ability. In addition, compared to placement of African American students, mainstream white representation in services for mild, moderate, and severe intellectual disabilities is below what would be expected based on genetic and normal human variation (Ford, Grantham, & Whiting, 2008). The figures indicating discriminate disproportionality are statistically significant even when accounting for severe variations in access to prenatal health services, differences in nutrition, and early childhood exposure to lead and other environmental pollutants. As seen in Table 8, as of 2002, African American, Hispanic/Latino, and American Indian students remain poorly represented in gifted education, especially CLD males (Ford et al., 2008).

**Table 8**    Data From Elementary and Secondary School Civil Rights Compliance Report

| Race/ethnicity | School Enrollment | | Gifted Enrollment | | Total | |
|---|---|---|---|---|---|---|
| | Percent Female | Percent Male | Percent Female | Percent Male | Percent School District | Percent Gifted and Talented |
| American Indian/Alaskan Native | 0.59 | 0.62 | 0.49 | 0.44 | 1.21 | 0.93 |
| Black | 8.46 | 8.70 | 4.78 | 3.65 | 17.16 | 8.43 |
| Hispanic/Latino | 8.67 | 9.12 | 5.36 | 5.05 | 17.80 | 10.41 |
| Asian/Pacific Islander | 2.14 | 2.28 | 3.65 | 3.43 | 4.42 | 7.64 |
| White | 28.81 | 30.61 | 36.71 | 35.88 | 59.42 | 72.59 |
| Total | 48.67 | 51.33 | 50.99 | 48.45 | 100.00 | 100.00 |

*Source:* US Department of Education, 2002.

# LEARNING DISABILITIES

In some instances, behaviors that educators initially believe indicate learning disabilities may be typical and normal for a specific cultural or linguistic background as a by-product of the acculturative process, including second language acquisition. When a CLD child is referred for suspected learning disabilities, the child's native culture and language, as well as stage of acculturation, must be considered. Knowledge of sociocultural considerations may help educators reduce unnecessary referrals and bias in making decisions about special education placement. Although limited English proficient students tend to be underrepresented in special education overall, they are over-represented in specific disability categories, including learning disabilities and speech/language impairments (Ortiz, 2010). Ortiz and Maldonado-Colon (1986) concluded that distinguishing linguistic and cultural differences from disabilities is difficult because students with disabilities and students with limited English proficiency share many of the same characteristics.

There are several reasons why data on culturally and linguistically different children may be misinterpreted. First, few of those involved in the decision-making process are knowledgeable about the normal learning patterns of second language acquisition (Rueda & Mercer, 1985) or the normal behavior patterns in stages of acculturation (Collier, 1985; Padilla, 1980). One of the forms of acculturation, that of assimilation, is commonly mistaken for the entire process. However, assimilation, in which the native culture (C1) is completely replaced by the second culture (C2), rarely happens. The more common outcome of acculturation is the integration of elements of the new culture with elements of the native culture, a blending of C1 and C2 elements. There is a clear need to help educators understand that many potentially troubling behaviors of culturally and linguistically different children are normal and should be anticipated given their cultural, linguistic, and acculturational backgrounds. Educators who are making placement decisions need information on the cultural, linguistic, and acculturational characteristics of the CLD children they work with, which means that they must seek out information about the particular cultural groups and apply these characteristics in individual cases.

Table 9 shows four areas that are characteristic of specific learning disabilities and outlines various cultural, linguistic, and acculturational factors

**Table 9**  Sociocultural Factors and Characteristics of Learning Disabilities

| ACADEMIC | | PSYCHOLOGICAL | |
|---|---|---|---|
| **Achievement Below Ability** | **Receptive and Expressive Language Deficits** | **Behavior Problems: Attention, Activity, Emotionality** | **Problems Associated With Cognitive and Learning Strategies** |
| • Experiential differences<br>• Group vs. individual<br>• Expectations<br>• Acculturative stage | • Linguistic differences<br>• Discourse patterns<br>• Limited English<br>• Limited native language<br>• Second language acquisition stage<br>• Nonverbal and sociolinguistic differences<br>• Hearing acuity vs. utility | • Psychodynamics of acculturation<br>• Interaction patterns<br>• Anxiety<br>• Persistence<br>• Discrimination<br>• Gender role expectations<br>• Survival skills<br>• Tempo | • Different perceptual categorization<br>• Orthographic differences<br>• Different cognitive learning styles:<br>  ○ Field<br>  ○ Tolerance<br>  ○ Categorization<br>  ○ Locus of control<br>  ○ Cognitive learning strategy differences |

to consider when referring CLD children. Consistent application of the suggestions that follow decreases inappropriate placement of culturally and linguistically different children in learning disabilities classes, improves instruction, and provides better understanding of their unique learning and behavior needs.

Behaviors used as indicators of specific learning disabilities are similar to typical and normal behaviors associated with acculturation and various cultural and linguistic differences. Educators involved in referral and placement decisions need to consider these characteristics in relation to the child's culture, language, and level of acculturation. As a first step, teachers should familiarize themselves with the particular cultural and linguistic backgrounds of their students. This familiarization, and awareness of acculturative considerations, can be facilitated by consultation with specialists in cross-cultural communication, acculturation, ESL, and bilingual education. Knowledge of the CLD child's cultural and linguistic background, consideration of the socio-cultural and acculturational factors described here, and application of the suggested interventions should help decrease inappropriate referral and placement of CLD children and provide more effective instruction to meet their unique educational needs.

The criteria for placement in special education as learning disabled are very specific: The student does not achieve commensurate with age or ability level when provided with appropriate learning experiences; there is a severe discrepancy between achievement and intellectual ability in one or more areas, including math, reading, writing, and language; and the discrepancy is not primarily the result of a sensory or organic impairment, mental retardation, emotional or behavioral disorders, or environmental, cultural, or economic disadvantage.

## SERVICE MODELS IN SPECIAL EDUCATION

In 2003, the Federal Office of English Language Acquisition reported that there was evidence of increasing instances of underrepresentation of limited English proficient students overall in special education categories (Ortiz & Maldonado-Colon, 2008), as school districts struggled to comply with regulations that required documentation demonstrating that presenting problems in learning were not due to the limited English of the learner. As noted by Ortiz (2010), current data indicates over-representation of limited English proficient speakers in learning disabilities and speech language impairments.

The drop in placement rates among mainstream white student enrollment in 2006, after the reauthorization of the Individuals with Disabilities Education Act of 2004, put even more pressure on districts to tighten up their identification and assessment procedures within the public K-12 system, especially those involving at-risk, diverse, and limited English proficient students with learning and behavior problems. Figure 27 illustrates the contrasting placement discrepancies found among CLD populations in 2006.

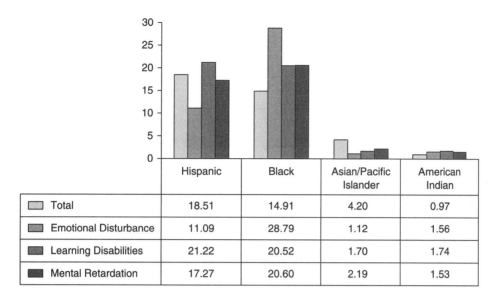

| | Hispanic | Black | Asian/Pacific Islander | American Indian |
|---|---|---|---|---|
| Total | 18.51 | 14.91 | 4.20 | 0.97 |
| Emotional Disturbance | 11.09 | 28.79 | 1.12 | 1.56 |
| Learning Disabilities | 21.22 | 20.52 | 1.70 | 1.74 |
| Mental Retardation | 17.27 | 20.60 | 2.19 | 1.53 |

**Figure 27**  Disproportionality in Special Education Placement, 2006

## INTEGRATING SPECIAL NEEDS AND CLDE NEEDS

A concern when planning services for CLDE students with disabilities who are also limited English proficient is how to balance language learning and acculturation needs with special learning needs; Given the length of time needed to develop the level of fluency for academic success in content areas, the cyclical nature of the acculturation adaptation process, and the individual learning issues of particular exceptional conditions, designing an effective integrated service plan for a CLDE student can be very challenging.

Table 10 represents a framework for addressing and balancing these needs. Across the top are listed descriptive levels of language acquisition, from preproduction to advanced fluency. The descriptions of language acquisition are adapted from Krashen (1981). Down the left hand column are degree of attention and assistance designed to address the exceptional individualized needs of the student. The staffing team selects the column heading that most closely matches the language acquisition level of the CLDE student under discussion. The table showing the language levels was included in Chapter 2 and would be used at each stage to monitor whether or not the CLDE student is making normal and adequate progress in language acquisition.

For very limited English speaking students with serious assistance needs, some portion of the school day could be spent in a special classroom setting (i.e., a setting in which their specific assistance needs and their specific second language learning and acculturation needs can be addressed in a combined intensive setting). In other words, the CLDE students with special needs are given instruction specific to their language

**Table 10**   Integration of Services Framework

| | Preproduction | Early Production | Speech Emergence | Intermediate Fluency | Intermediate Advanced Fluency | Advanced Fluency |
|---|---|---|---|---|---|---|
| Needs total assistance | | | | | | |
| Needs a great deal of assistance | | | | | | |
| Needs a lot of assistance | | | | | | |
| Has a moderate level of needs | | | | | | |
| Has moderate but specific needs | | | | | | |
| Has specific need to be addressed | | | | | | |
| Needs minimal assistance | | | | | | |

learning and special needs. In some states, these instructional settings are staffed by cross-certificated education personnel (e.g., a licensed special educator who is bilingual and certificated in English as a second language instruction). This setting may also be staffed by a trained bilingual professional working with a trained monolingual special educator or similar configuration of personnel.

For students of very limited English with only moderate assistance needs, a bilingual special educator and bilingual ESL teacher work in conjunction with general classroom personnel to provide targeted assistance within the integrated classroom. In some states, this is done with itinerant professionals who meet regularly with classroom teachers to coach and co-plan lessons.

For students with moderate English speaking proficiency (at least speech emergence) and with moderate assistance needs, a portion of their school day could be spent in a combination of small group assistance and in-class assistance with a specialist (i.e., a *push-in* or *plug-in* setting). For students of moderate proficiency and with moderate but specific needs, a portion of their day may consist of push-in or plug-in assistance from a specialist within their classroom setting. Students with high proficiency in English and a variety of special education needs can generally be served within an inclusive integrated regular classroom. This is typical of limited English proficient students who are in wheelchairs or are otherwise covered by 504 services. Different combinations of special need, language proficiency, acculturation and language learning needs may be planned for by considering their intersection on the framework shown in Table 10. In some districts with access to cross-trained personnel, services are leveraged by level of need for special education services and level of need for culturally and linguistically tailored services. For example, at the highest level of need in both exceptionality and culture or language, a certificated bilingual special educator will work with the CLDE special education student most of the day, while a student with moderate needs would be served within the general classroom with daily visits from a bilingual ELL specialist and special educator trained in working with CLDE students who meet and coordinate with the classroom teacher.

In conclusion, Step 6 of the PRISIM process of problem solving for CLDE students is focused on identifying a student's special individualized instructional needs and outlining a monitoring and service plan. If special education services are appropriate, the student is placed in a program that meets the student's unique instructional needs and an IEP is developed. The IEP must include instructional accommodations that address the student's diverse language and culture needs in interaction with the student's special needs.

## JOSÉ CASE STUDY

When we last left him, José had shown through his response during the intensive individualized intervention that he has the capacity to learn academic content in all areas and to become a successful reader in both English and Spanish. However, the team was worried about the achievement gap between him and his CLDE peers and that it took so much support and effort to bring his learning and behavior closer to his peers. Under IDEA, before proceeding with a formal evaluation, the district must document that the CLDE student's learning and behavior problems are not primarily due to his proficiency in English and that his second language learning are proceeding within in a normal range of acquisition. The team was able to document this by showing that José progressed from non-English speaking to a low intermediate fluency level with just over 24 months of direct instruction. They also documented all of the interventions that had been implemented and José's response to them, as shown on Table 11. This included all instructional interventions from Tier 1 and 2, as well as those from Tier 3, that had been implemented over the course of two months during his second year and beginning his third year in the school district.

**Table 11**  Example of Framework for Integrating José's Plan

| | Preproduction | Early Production | Speech Emergence | Intermediate Fluency | Intermediate Advanced Fluency | Advanced Fluency |
|---|---|---|---|---|---|---|
| Needs total assistance | | | | | | |
| Needs a great deal of assistance | | | José's English proficiency | José's Spanish proficiency | | |
| Needs a lot of assistance | | | | | | |
| Has a moderate level of needs | | | | | | |
| Has moderate but specific needs | | | | | | |
| Has specific need to be addressed | | | Bilingual counselor working with classroom teacher and ELL personnel | | | |
| Needs minimal assistance | | | | | | |
| Needs no special assistance | | | | | | |

## PRISIM 6 Tier 4 Integrated Services

After consulting with the school psychologist, counselor, social worker, special education teacher, and principal, the team decided further evaluation of José's behavior and self-control were warranted. His difficulty working without one-on-one guidance was discussed with his family, and further testing was conducted by a bilingual team. His parents supported this and explained that his grandmother was getting increasingly frustrated with his behavior at home as well as his siblings' reports of how he behaved at school. An individualized plan with CLDE services was developed. The framework for José's service plan is shown in Table 11, with his language level in English and Spanish in conjunction with his need for some specific behavior modification assistance indicated by the shaded area.

# Maintaining and Sustaining 7 CLDE Programs

**PRISIM Step 7. Maintaining and Sustaining Programs for CLDE Students**

*Verifying qualifications of bilingual CLDE personnel and paraprofessionals involved in this comprehensive service structure, as described under current US federal law. Continuous monitoring and dynamic service placement across all tiers. Building and sustaining the most effective elements of such problem-solving with progress-monitoring programs across all levels of instruction.*

After addressing disproportionality in the referral and placement of diverse learners, the issue of maintaining appropriate services still remains. As noted in Chapter 6, some districts have access to cross-trained personnel and some do not. What do schools do with students who are limited English proficient *and* have some particular exceptionality when the schools have limited access to cross-trained and multi-licensed specialists? There are very few bilingual special educators generally available in public or private school districts. In a recent study, Mazur and Givens (2004) identified only seven institutions of higher education in the United States that have professional licensure programs in bilingual special education and even fewer programs that produce bilingual school psychologists. Moreover, having bilingual special education professionals on staff does not automatically address the issue of serving many languages and cultures in a single instructional setting. Schools serving diverse learners with exceptionalities who are limited English proficient must develop integrated service plans using their current staffing configurations, usually a monolingual special educator, a monolingual school psychologist, a monolingual classroom teacher, and a monolingual or bilingual English as a second language teacher. This team faces unique challenges in delivering integrated special education services that also provide for the student's language acquisition needs.

## SERVICE OPTIONS

The IEP must be developed in such a way that all of the culture, acculturation, and language acquisition needs of the culturally and linguistically diverse exceptional (CLDE) student are addressed and monitored in the context of the presenting problem or exceptionality. The team members who develop the IEP must identify who will provide which services and in what languages and communication contexts content instruction will occur. If the special educator is bilingual in the CLDE student's language and dialect or has training in ESL instructional approaches, he or she can provide both special education and language acquisition support. If the classroom teacher is bilingual or has training in ESL, he or she can provide the language acquisition support while the student is mainstreamed; however, what usually occurs is that bilingual ESL personnel provide support within the special education and regular classroom. Depending on the particular level of assistance needed, this may be done as pull-out or push-in services. Pull-out ESL is a program in which CLDE students are pulled out of regular, mainstream or special classrooms for special instruction in English as a second language, while in push-in ESL instruction, the ESL teacher enters the special or mainstream classroom to work with CLDE students (E. A. Baker, 2000). Without intensive coordination between all teachers, this separation of focus may not adequately or effectively address the CLDE special education student's unique complex of needs.

In addition, the exceptionality of the CLDE student may impact his or her capacity to acquire English to the most advanced proficiency levels. The team developing the IEP will need to identify specific English proficiency goals for the CLDE students that are appropriate to the specific identified disabling condition. Within the increasingly popular *dual language* programs found in many states, the team will need to address how the IEP is to be implemented within the context of the dual, two-way, language program offered in the CLDE student's school.

An additional concern with this comprehensive service structure is whether or not the bilingual ESL personnel are certificated teachers or paraprofessionals. Under current US federal law, all school personnel who deliver direct instruction and instructional support must be "highly qualified." In practice, there is great variation in how well-prepared either professionals or paraprofessionals are to work with exceptional students who are limited English proficient. This is especially an issue with paraprofessionals whose primary duties are translation or interpretation. Under current IDEA 2004 legislation, interpreters and translators are not required to be highly qualified.

There are a number of critical problems in recruiting and retaining highly qualified education professionals who are skilled in working effectively with CLDE students. In 2008, national public school enrollment exceeded 54 million, and it is estimated that nationwide some 2.2 million teachers will be needed in the next 10 years because of teacher attrition and retirement and increased student enrollment. In high-poverty urban and rural districts alone, more than 700,000 new teachers will be needed in the next 10 years (National Center for Education Statistics, 1993). Nationwide enrollment in elementary schools is expected to increase by 17% and in high schools by 26%. In a typical year, an estimated 6% of the nation's teaching force leaves the profession and more than 7% changes schools. Twenty percent of all new hires leave teaching within three years (National Center for Education Statistics, 1993). In urban districts, close to 50% of newcomers abandon the profession during their first five years of teaching (Darling-Hammond & Sclan, 1996). Minority students make up 33% of enrollment in US public schools, while the total of minority teachers reaches just 13.5%, and about 42% of public schools in the United States have no minority teachers at all. By the mid-21st century, the percentage of minority teachers is expected to shrink to an all-time low of 5%, while 41% of US American students will be minorities (National Center for Education Statistics, 2000). The greatest teaching shortages are in bilingual and special education, mathematics, science (particularly the physical sciences), computer science, English-as-a-Second-Language, and foreign languages (American Association for Employment in Education, 2008).

The following facts, drawn from Department of Education surveys, further demonstrate the magnitude of this personnel shortage in the fields of special education and bilingual and ESL education.

Only 10% of teachers working with LEP students are certified in bilingual education and/or ESL (Council of Chief State School Officers, 1991).

"Thirty-seven percent of school administrators who had vacancies in ESL or bilingual education found them 'very difficult or impossible to fill'" (National Research Council, 1997, p. 252).

"Teacher placement officers ranked bilingual education as the field with the highest degree of teacher shortage and the highest demand" (National Research Council, 1997, p. 252).

Fradd, Baca, and Collier (1996) and Mazur and Givens (2004) found that there are very few teacher preparation programs training personnel for bilingual special education programs. Mazur and Givens surveyed 530 National Council for Accreditation of Teacher Education (NCATE) approved teacher preparation programs at colleges and universities across the United States; out of the 47% that responded, fewer than 5% had a program to prepare bilingual special educators to work with CLDE students. Over 46% of respondents to the Mazur and Givens study stated that there was a need for a teacher preparation program to prepare bilingual special educators to work with CLDE students but cited lack of resources or staff to develop such a program.

There was a time when CLD students were given very little or no special consideration in US schools. Today, however, because of hard fought legislative and judicial battles, the opportunity for CLD students to receive a high quality education has improved considerably. Educators today have developed a greater awareness of the needs of CLD students. In addition, educators have developed a measure of new knowledge and expertise in first- and second-language development and instruction. Nevertheless, this new capacity to better educate the CLD student is not well established nor evenly distributed among educators. Most regular classroom teachers and administrators are not equipped with this new knowledge and expertise, and most schools of education do not provide or require students to take courses in language minority education. This newly established capacity and expertise is limited to a relatively small number of university and public school specialists who work specifically in language minority programs, such as bilingual education and English as a Second Language (ESL).

## TEACHER PREPARATION

Using data from several states, researchers have begun drawing some important conclusions about teacher preparation (Hannaway & Kimball, 1997). It has been found that teacher effectiveness varies enormously within schools and districts, although teachers are consistently weakest in their first year or two. After those first few years, the path a teacher took into the classroom seems to make little difference, and the value of experience does not build in equal increments with years on the job. Also, a few good teachers in a row can significantly raise students' achievement, concludes Jane Hannaway, the principal investigator for the National Center for Analysis of Longitudinal Data in Education Research, or CALDER, at the Urban Institute (Hannaway & Kimball, 1997).

Little (1993) also emphasized that when professional development takes teachers' experiences and work contexts seriously from its inception, when it considers teachers as more than consumers of knowledge but also as actively engaged in inquiry, and when it aims for professional growth and colleagueship, teachers are more likely to engage intellectually, socially, and emotionally with ideas, materials, and their work peers. Put simply, professional development that addresses the specific, daily needs of teachers and their students is more likely to produce changes in teachers' practice (Joyce & Showers, 1982). Furthermore, teachers benefit most "when their learning is reinforced over time through repeated and varied exposure to ideas and through interactions with colleagues, who can act as a resource for each other's learning" (Cohen & Hill, 2001 as cited in Knapp, 2003, p. 121; see also Desimone, Garet, Birman, Porter, & Yoon, 2002). Unfortunately, this is not generally the mode in teacher preparation and licensure programs, and most public school districts resort to inservice training of education personnel, variations on what are sometimes called *retraining*, *untraining*, or *retreading* programs after teachers receive their initial licensure to teach from colleges and universities. The best of these programs include peer coaching and learning communities within school districts. If orchestrated long-term, and focused on ongoing collaboration between professionals around a common problem of practice that they deem important, coaching and collaborative learning activities among practitioners can result in powerful and sustainable professional development that directly and significantly impacts student learning.

Coaching utilizes a variety of pathways to help teachers, school leaders, and district leaders build school capacity for sustained change and improvement (Neufeld & Roper, 2003). Principals and central office staff, for instance, may use leadership coaches to guide their classroom walkthroughs or planning meetings. At the classroom level, instructional coaching might look different; it could take the form of one-on-one support for teachers or guided observation and debriefing of their colleagues' teaching. Due to the varied roles and responsibilities of the job, however, defining coaches' work has proven difficult for researchers (Taylor, 2008). Most definitions of coaching offer general approximations of what coaches do, such as, "use conversation skills, listening, curiosity, compassion, expertise, and problem solving to help others move toward their goals, hopes, and dreams" (McNeil & Klink, 2004, p. 1) or "nonsupervisory/nonevaluative individualized guidance and support that takes place directly within the instructional setting" (Taylor, 2008, p. 12). And while ambiguous, it is possible that these generic definitions are the closest approximation to what coaches do, given the highly nuanced nature of the work. Coaching involves humans—in all of their individuality and unpredictability—who must navigate difficult issues of trust, communication, and inevitable differences of opinion.

What is needed in effective teacher preparation is a blend of preservice and inservice models that benefit educators by (1) promoting active reflection on current practices (Garmston, Linder, & Whitaker, 1993; Joyce & Showers, 1982; Stein & D'Amico, 2002); (2) teaching educators how to apply new concepts to their unique work environments (Neufeld & Roper, 2003; Showers & Joyce, 1996); (3) building generative communities of practice (Lowenhaupt & McKinney, 2007; Showers, 1985); and (4) fostering professionalism among colleagues (Garmston, 1987). To summarize, it is important to reframe teacher preparation as part of a greater problem of practice that all educators struggle with: How to simultaneously push all students to their potential and cultivate their desire to learn? Achieving this with CLDE students who may also be limited English proficient is partly linked to the changing legal and context within our school systems. Teacher preparation programs must include the training of all education professionals concerning the current guidelines for CLDE students contained within the reauthorized IDEA.

The 2004 reauthorization of IDEA added several specific guidelines that addressed language and culture issues when identifying, assessing, and developing instructional plans for limited English proficient students with special needs. Following is a summary of some of the key provisions addressing LEP concerns:

1. The public agency shall make reasonable efforts to ensure that the parents understand, and are able to participate in, any group decisions relating to the educational placement of their child, including arranging for an interpreter for parents with deafness or whose native language is other than English. [§300.501(c)(5)]

2. In considering the child's language needs (as they relate to the child's IEP), if the IEP team determines that the child needs a particular device or service (including an intervention, accommodation, or other program modification) in order for the child to receive Free and Appropriate Public Education (FAPE), the team must include a statement to that effect in the child's IEP. [§300.346(a)(2)(ii) and §300.346(b) and (c)]

3. For an LEP child with a disability, the IEP must address whether the special education and related services that the child needs will be provided in a language other than English. [§300.346(a)(2)(ii) and §300.346(b) and (c)]

4. Each public agency must ensure that tests and other evaluation materials used to assess a child under Part B of IDEA

   a. are selected and administered so as not to be discriminatory on a racial or cultural basis; and

   b. are provided and administered in the child's native language or other mode of communication, unless it is clearly not feasible to do so. [§300.532(a)]

5. Each public agency must also ensure that materials and procedures used to assess a child with limited English proficiency are selected and administered to ensure that they measure the extent to which the child has a disability and needs special education rather than measuring the child's English language skills. [§300.532(a)]

6. Under Title VI of the Civil Rights Act of 1964:

   a. In order to properly evaluate a child who may be limited English proficient, a public agency should assess the child's proficiency in English as well as in his or her native language to distinguish language proficiency from disability needs. [§300.534(b)(1)]

7. In some situations, there may be no one on the staff of the public agency who is able to administer a test or other evaluation in the child's native language, but an appropriate individual is available in the surrounding area. [§300.345]. In that case, a public agency could identify an individual in the surrounding area who is able to administer a test or other evaluation in the child's native language, including contacting neighboring school districts, local universities, and professional organizations. [§300.345]

8. A child may not be determined to be eligible under Part B if the determinant factor for that eligibility determination is the child's lack of instruction in reading or math or the child's limited English proficiency and the child does not otherwise meet the eligibility criteria for a "child with a disability." [§300.534(b)(1)]

These provisions are only some of the changes in the reauthorized IDEA that aim to provide a more effective method of identifying specific learning and behavior disabilities in CLDE students. In order to comply with the requirements of IDEA, teachers should possess certain skills and competencies related to working with CLDE students.

# SPECIFIC SKILLS AND COMPETENCIES FOR TEACHERS

The author has compiled a recommended list of skills and competencies that education professionals should have in order to work most effectively with CLDE students in today's classrooms. These competencies and skills facilitate the implementation of the PRISIM approach discussed in the Introduction:

1. The teacher accurately demonstrates knowledge of the content area and approved curriculum.
   a. Utilizes and enhances approved curriculum
   b. Gives clear explanations relating to lesson content and procedure
   c. Communicates accurately in the content area
   d. Shows interrelatedness of one content area to another
   e. Works as a team with parents and special education teachers to learn what skills a child needs and to provide the best teaching approach
   f. Maintains flexibility and a high tolerance for ambiguity

2. Teacher appropriately utilizes a variety of teaching methods and resources for each area and each student taught.
   a. Realizes that every child in the class is the teacher's personal responsibility (Teachers need to find out how to work with each child rather than assuming someone else will tell them how to educate the child.)
   b. Knows a variety of instructional strategies and how to use them effectively (This includes the ability to adapt materials and rewrite objectives for a child's needs.)
   c. Provides opportunities for students to work independently, in small groups, and in large groups, as appropriate
   d. Uses a variety of methods, such as demonstrations, lectures, student-initiated work, group work, questioning, independent practice, and so on, as appropriate
   e. Uses a variety of resources such as field trips, supplemental printed materials, and manipulatives, as appropriate
   f. Provides opportunities for students to apply, practice, and demonstrate knowledge and skills learned through various modalities
   g. Uses sheltered instruction strategies
   h. Supports learning of the second language through content
   i. Engages students in cooperative learning
   j. Uses cross-age and peer tutoring

    k. Integrates native English speakers with English language learners for instructional purposes

    l. Uses interdisciplinary, thematic units

   m. Uses technology to enhance language learning and concept understanding

3. The teacher communicates with and obtains feedback from students in a manner that enhances student learning and understanding.

    a. Is able to modify assignments for students and design classroom activities with many levels, so that all students have a part (This teaching skill can apply not just at the elementary or secondary level, but at the college level as well. It will mean more activity-based teaching rather than seat-based teaching.)

    b. Explains or demonstrates the relevance of topics and activities

    c. Communicates to students the instructional intent, directions, or plan at the appropriate time

    d. Establishes and states expectations for student performance

    e. Clarifies actions, directions, and explanations when students do not understand

    f. Actively solicits communication from students about their learning

    g. Communicates regularly with students about their progress

4. The teacher comprehends the principles of student growth, development, and learning, and applies them appropriately.

    a. Is able to take advantage of children's individual interests and use their internal motivation for developing needed skills

    b. Views each child in the class as an opportunity to become a better teacher, rather than as a problem to be coped with or have someone else fix

    c. Has knowledge of second language acquisition

    d. Is familiar with whole-language approaches to integrate oral language development with writing, reading, and listening

    e. Affirms and builds on student's native language as much as possible

    f. Employs and instructs students in the use of cognitive thinking skills such as critical thinking, problem solving, divergent thinking, inquiry, and decision making

    g. Uses teaching techniques, materials, and media that address student learning levels, rates, and styles

    h. Uses resources such as community service agencies, school personnel, and parents to meet students' learning levels, rates, and styles

5. The teacher effectively utilizes student assessment techniques and procedures.

    a. Is able to set high but alternative expectations that are suitable for the students (e.g., developing alternative assessments)

b. Is able to make appropriate expectations for each student, regardless of the student's capabilities

c. Is able to problem-solve and informally assess the skills a student needs (rather than relying solely on standardized curriculum)

d. Uses a variety of assessment tools and strategies, as appropriate

e. Properly assesses English language learners

f. Uses information gained from ongoing assessment for remediation and instructional planning

g. Maintains documentation of student progress

h. Communicates student progress with students and families in a timely manner

6. The teacher manages the educational setting in a manner that promotes positive student behavior and a safe and healthy environment.

a. Is able to value all kinds of skills that students bring to a class, not just the academic skills; moreover, teachers must demonstrate and make explicit that in their classrooms, they value all skills, even if they are not of clear value in the whole school

b. Promotes respect for students of all backgrounds

c. Develops an environment where all students feel equally accepted, welcomed, and challenged

d. Serves as a model for constructive behavior patterns

e. Executes routine tasks effectively and efficiently

f. Establishes and states expectations for student behavior

g. Handles transitions effectively

h. Has materials and media ready to use

i. Minimizes distractions and interruptions

j. Manages student behavior effectively and appropriately

k. Identifies hazards, assesses risks, and takes appropriate action

7. The teacher recognizes student diversity and creates an atmosphere conducive to the promotion of positive student involvement and self-concept.

a. Is able to promote daily success for all students. (Teachers have to work to counteract the message all students get when certain students are continually taken out of class for special work.)

b. Promotes respect for students of all backgrounds

c. Develops an environment where all students feel equally accepted, welcomed, and challenged

d. Prevents and addresses issues of intolerance, prejudice, and bias

e. Promotes students' interest in learning about different cultures, languages, and lifestyles

f. Is familiar with a wide range of materials and literature from different cultures and periods in history to enrich the curriculum

g. Is familiar with techniques to integrate students' culture and experiences into the curriculum

h. Demonstrates sensitivity and responsiveness to the personal ideas, needs, interests, and feelings of students

i. Acknowledges student performance and achievement

j. Acknowledges that every student can learn

k. Provides opportunities for each student to succeed

l. Provides students with opportunities for active involvement and creativity

m. Provides opportunities for students to be responsible for their own behavior and learning

n. Promotes positive student-teacher relationships

o. Encourages high student expectations

p. Demonstrates an awareness and respect for each student's background, experience, and culture

8. The teacher demonstrates a willingness to examine and implement change, as appropriate.

a. Seeks out information on methodology, research, and current trends in education to enhance and improve the quality of learning

b. Implements a variety of strategies to enhance learning

c. Recognizes that change entails risks and modifications may be needed

9. The teacher works productively with colleagues, parents, and community members.

a. Communicates with parents on a regular basis

b. Effectively communicates with parents from diverse backgrounds

c. Promotes parental involvement of parents of diverse backgrounds

d. Integrates community "funds of knowledge" (Gonzalez et al., 1993) into the curriculum

e. Collaborates with colleagues

f. Uses conflict resolving strategies when necessary

g. Involves parents and community in the learning environment

h. Communicates in a professional manner with colleagues, parents, and community members regarding educational matters

In addition, all education personnel and persons working in situations where bilingual interpreting and translation is used need training and development. There are linguistic, cultural, and professional competencies that must be part of the recruitment and preparation of bilingual persons preparing to become interpreters or translators. The linguistic competencies for translators and interpreters include the following:

- The ability to understand and converse in the Ll and the L2 with a high degree of proficiency
- The ability to understand and use reading and writing skills in the L1 and the L2 with a high degree of proficiency
- The ability to say the same thing in different ways
- The ability to adjust to different levels of language usage (colloquial or more formal dialectical variations, social and academic language)
- The capacity to switch with familiarity between different types of interpretation and translation
- The ability to remember information
- Knowledge of technical educational terminology
- Knowledge of the culture of the language interpreted or translated

Cultural competencies must also be an expected outcome of training and staff development for interpreters and translators. These cultural competencies include, but are not limited to, the following:

1. An understanding of cross-cultural interaction patterns

2. An ability to use cross-cultural communication strategies effectively

3. An understanding of subgroups within various cultures

4. An understanding of acceptable and expected behaviors within both C1 and C2 interactions

There are also competencies associated with learning to perform as an education professional, including confidentiality, ethics, and expectations of the school system and other education professionals. Preparation, orientation, and training of translators and interpreters for special education assistance must include training in these competency expectations. These educational competencies include the following:

1. The ability to maintain professional conduct in all situations

2. The ability to maintain and to explain the need for confidentiality

3. The ability to remain impartial and neutral

4. The ability to be straightforward, to not accept an assignment beyond one's capabilities, and to be able to ask for help or clarification when necessary

5. The capacity to display respect for the authority of the administrator or the diagnostician

6. The ability to work as a part of the team with the education staff

Sometimes school districts with extensive needs for interpreting and translating have an extensive and comprehensive training program for interpreters and translators that also includes courses in child development, tests and measurements, and an orientation to educational theory. The interpreter or translator also needs to learn to work well with the school psychologist, diagnostician, special educator, and other education professionals he or she may be assisting. These comprehensive interpreter- or translator-training programs are usually integrated into career ladder and professional development programs that prepare bilingual and ESL certificated personnel.

There are also training needs related to preparing education professionals of all backgrounds to work with an interpreter or translator. This training is usually offered through inservice staff development programs and is sometimes part of a general district professional development plan. The school professional working with an interpreter or translator needs the ability to plan and implement pre- and postdiagnostic conferences with the interpreter or translator. He or she will need to orient and train the interpreter or translator as to the particular purpose and procedures appropriate to the formal testing, interviews, observations, and so on, that will be carried out.

The school professional also needs preparation in group and individual interaction dynamics. He or she needs to be able to establish rapport with all participants in the cross-cultural and cross-lingual interaction. This usually involves some training in cross-cultural communication techniques and strategies. Knowledge of the methods and techniques of interpretation and translation is also useful.

School professionals who are to work with an interpreter must be aware of and sensitive to the kinds of information loss that are inherent in the interpretation procedure (e.g., omissions, additions, substitutions). They must also have an understanding of the limitations of formal tests administered using an interpreter or translator. Given these limitations, the professional must become proficient in using observation of the student's responses to testing, language, behavior, and nonverbal communication.

## Training Paraprofessionals as Interpreters and Translators

Implicit in selecting and using interpreters and translators is assuring that they receive appropriate training and preparation. The key is to provide training before student testing and to review after testing. Translating, especially in an evaluative capacity, can be a very difficult task, and it usually requires training for the interpreter in all phases of assessment because the interpreter should be involved in the total assessment process, including test modification. The translation of a test instrument or any other material may be checked for validity by having another bilingual person translate the non-English version text back into English. This process is termed *back translation*. There will be slight variations, but the meaning should remain the same.

In addition to a high level of competency in all four language skills (listening, speaking, reading, writing), the interpreter should have some understanding of student development, language variation (dialects, language domains, etc.), and cross-cultural variables. Interpreters need training in the administration of tests, including how to transmit information about role playing, how to cue a student during assessment, how to prompt for responses, and how to probe for pertinent information or responses. Training in confidentiality is also essential. Competence and expertise will vary among interpreters, but what is essential in this important position is a highly developed sense of professional responsibility.

There are a number of special considerations for interpreters and translators; these include omissions, additions, common errors, substitutions, and transformations. Training of interpreters and translators must include how to avoid and self-correct for these problem areas when working cross-lingually.

**Omissions:** Interpreters and translators sometimes omit single words, phrases, or sentences. They may do this when they do not know the meaning of the words, phrases, or sentences or when the words cannot be translated. Omissions may also occur when the interpreter or translator cannot keep up with the pace of the speaker, cannot retain all the details, or has forgotten what was said.

**Additions:** Interpreters and translators sometimes add extra words, phrases, or entire sentences. They may do this when they wish to be more elaborate or when they editorialize. The interpreter or translator may add when they need to explain a difficult concept for which there is no equivalent in the other language.

**Substitutions:** Interpreters and translators sometimes use words, phrases, or sentences other than the specified ones. They may do this when they make an error or when they misunderstand the speaker. Substitutions also occur when interpreters or translators cannot keep up with the pace of the speaker and must formulate material based on the words that they have heard. The interpreter or translator may become confused about the words (e.g., homonyms) or fail to retrieve a specific word or phrase.

**Transformations:** Interpreters and translators sometimes change the word order of the statement, which could distort the meaning.

**Errors:** Some errors may occur due to unequal skill in the L1 or the L2. Some interpreters and translators may find it easier to interpret from L1 to L2 than from L2 to L1, and vice versa. Occasionally, errors may occur due to differences in style. Some interpreters and translators may change the meaning of the message through their personal style of intonation, facial expressions, and gestures.

## Interpersonal Training

Training on effective interpersonal communication and sensitivity to the linguistic and cultural characteristics of the home are also important elements when preparing translators and interpreters. In planning parental involvement activities, it is important to plan around the needs of the entire family, rather than to limit the focus narrowly to the needs of the child with disabilities or the needs of the parents. In thinking about the following parent involvement activities, it is always best to assume a family system's perspective to obtain the most positive results. Education professionals should provide parents with resources by collecting brochures and booklets (in both the L1 and the L2) about community resources; information concerning the various disabilities, written in layperson's terms; and services for care, counseling, disability-related services, adult education and training programs, associations, and clubs. School personnel should work with community leaders concerning the community's needs and goals. They may jointly organize supportive services for families or jointly plan activities for families and make home visits. Personal contact with the whole family is very important for bridging the home-school gap.

Through discussions with parents, school staff can plan an optimal day of the week, time, and place for the meeting. They should have a specific purpose in mind related to parent needs and goals. Parent leadership and involvement in the planning and implementation of events is critical. Examples of parent-child services are a reading center, a parent activity center, an information clearinghouse, and a phone help line.

To involve parents in their children's education, school personnel can invite parents to assist in the classroom with tutoring, special events (fairs, shows), or the donation of time or talent (cooking, sewing, translating, making needed classroom items). School personnel should communicate with the home and hold frequent informal parent conferences. Other forms of contact include sending home a "good work" folder of student work products or sending photographs or monthly letters reporting on class activities. Some schools send home books, tapes, or home activities to complete with parents. Some schools have parent education workshops where parents can learn about the school. Workshop themes can vary from ESL classes to role-playing interactions with administrators, teachers, paraprofessionals, and school clerical or secretarial staff to increase negotiation strategies available to parents.

In conclusion, building and sustaining the most effective elements of problem solving with progress monitoring programs across all levels of instruction is vital to improving the education of culturally and linguistically diverse learners, including those with exceptionalities. Current US federal law now requires teachers and other educational staff to balance the disability and language needs of CLDE students; however, there are many obstacles to fully meeting those standards. A lack of adequate funds, teacher preparation programs, and qualified professionals trained to work with CLDE students makes it challenging to comply with legislative requirements.

As a response to this situation, the author proposes the PRISIM model and its seven-step process for separating difference from disability. By incorporating RTI and RTII methodology into instruction and interventions for culturally and linguistically diverse learners, the model provides steps to assure that CLDE students receive the free and appropriate public education (FAPE) guaranteed to them by current legislation. It also reduces the number of CLDE students who are disproportionately identified (either under or over) for special services. Developing and consistently implementing a model such as PRISIM or RTI/RTII that includes continuous problem solving with progress monitoring and dynamic instruction and instructional intervention across all levels of instruction holds much promise for rectifying the educational and service inequities currently present in US American schools for culturally and linguistically diverse learners.

# JOSÉ CASE STUDY

In the best of all possible worlds, José's family would have access to a full range of multilingual or multicultural community and support services, and personnel working with José would have access to all necessary resources, materials, books, media, and support services within the framework of a top-of-the-line multilanguage and literacy-in-the-content-areas program. However, in reality, José would be served by a combination of the most effective materials, programs, and personnel the district has available.

## PRISIM 7 Integrated Services, Teaching, and Monitoring Across all Areas

The design and maintenance of a comprehensive integrated service plan for José started with building the foundation for effective learning. Therefore, at Step 1 of an integrated plan for José, the goal for the receiving school district was to

- Promote and sustain José's access to safety, food, clothing, and shelter
- Assure quality preparation of effective education professionals and support staff who will be working with José
- Maintain the adequacy of school facilities and resources available to José and his family
- Monitor and sustain consistent use of culturally and linguistically responsive, evidence-based practices when working with José
- Maintain supportive responsive relationships between José and school personnel

Also at Step 1, the district continued training education personnel in cultural competence and facilitating social justice and language acquisition of linguistically diverse learners and their families.

Step 2 in a comprehensive and sustainable plan for José was to identify the following four information areas, and based on this, for classroom personnel to use instructional strategies that maximized Jose's strengths and facilitated his adaptation to the curriculum and procedures used in the school:

1. José's cultural experience and language background

2. Level of language proficiency in each of José's languages

3. José's level of acculturation as he entered the school district

4. Prior schooling and content achievement

5. José's strengths and resiliency areas

Differentiation of instruction with progress monitoring began at this point to facilitate the school instructional team's ability to initiate specific interventions as needs arose for José. Training in differentiation, language development, and cognitive learning strategies was provided across the district to all education personnel.

Step 3 in a sustainable plan for José was to continue the differentiation of instruction begun at Step 2 and to supplement it with small group implementation of specific strategies to address his emerging needs. A needs prioritization was completed and up-to-date information on his language acquisition, content learning, and level of acculturation was obtained. Strategies that were found to be effective for José at Step 3 might be used in the context of large group instruction. Strategy training of all personnel was provided with follow-up peer coaching. The progress monitoring process was used by the instructional team in the building to decide whether José needed more small group sessions, more intensive individualized sessions, or if he could return to full participation in his home classroom.

Step 4 in José's comprehensive plan occurred when the instructional team designed and implemented an intensive individualized instructional intervention plan with specifically targeted progress monitoring to determine José's response to intervention. Monitoring was conducted as well, and up-to-date information on his language acquisition, content learning, and level of acculturation was obtained. Strategies that were found to be effective for José at Step 4 might be used in the context of small group instruction, also. Strategy training of all personnel was provided with peer coaching by early adaptors. The progress monitoring process was used by the instructional team in the building to decide whether José needed to continue individualized intensive intervention, could be returned to small group sessions, or might return to full participation in his home classroom with the effective strategies. Effective strategies (i.e., the building blocks of learning for José) were seen as moveable and dynamic and not applicable within just one level of instruction. If a strategy was successful for José and he responded well to its use in an intervention, then education personnel working with José continued to use it. Documentation of the success of specific strategies was part of the progress monitoring across tiers that the team was carrying out.

Step 5 consisted of reviewing and analyzing the information gathered during the progress monitoring part of José's problem solving process. The team determined whether José required additional screening and assessment (formal referral) or whether sufficient progress had been documented to take José out of the intensive individualized intervention and place him back into a less intensive instructional setting.

At Step 6, an individualized plan was developed for José that included his language, acculturation, and content-learning needs. Education personnel working with José received *booster shot* training on the use of integrated strategies.

# Conclusion

Building and sustaining the most effective elements of problem solving with progress monitoring programs across all levels of instruction is vital to improving the education of culturally and linguistically diverse learners, including those with exceptionalities. Current U.S. federal law now requires teachers and other educational staff to balance the disability and language needs of CLD and CLDE students; however, there are many obstacles to fully meeting those standards. A lack of adequate funds, teacher preparation programs, and qualified professionals trained to work with CLD and CLDE students makes it challenging to comply with legislative requirements.

As a response to this situation, the author proposes the PRISIM model and its seven-step process for separating difference from disability. By incorporating RTI/RTII methodology into instruction and interventions for culturally and linguistically diverse learners, the model provides steps to assure that CLD students receive the free and appropriate education (FAPE) guaranteed to them by current legislation. It also reduces the number of CLD students who are disproportionately identified (either under or over) for special services. Developing and consistently implementing a model such as PRISIM and/or RTI/RTII that includes continuous problem solving with progress monitoring and dynamic instruction and instructional intervention across all levels of instruction holds much promise of rectifying the educational and service inequities currently present in U.S. American schools for culturally and linguistically diverse learners.

# Glossary

**accommodation.** Adapting language (spoken or written) to make it more understandable to second language learners. In assessment, accommodations may be made to the presentation, response method, setting, or timing/scheduling of the assessment.

**acculturation.** Acculturation is the process of adaptation to changes in our social, cultural, and linguistic environments.

**active processing strategy.** When applying the active processing strategy, students work through problems or tasks using a sequence of self-monitoring questions. Start by having the students in your class speak out loud with one another in small groups about the content and process of lessons they are learning following the steps in active processing.

**acquisition (versus learning).** Krashen states that acquisition amounts to a functional mastery of some aspect of a language, such as a word or grammar structure that you don't have to translate from your first language because you "just know it." To some extent acquisition is 'subconscious' or covert and learning is conscious or overt. Learning is a conscious process whereby we store information about a language in our minds, access it and use it consciously to translate to or from the target language. Language learners in typical settings perform both acquisition and learning simultaneously.

**additive bilingualism.** One of two contextual concepts which explain the possible outcomes of second language learning. Additive bilingualism occurs in an environment in which the addition of a second language and culture does not replace the first language and culture; rather, the first language/culture are promoted and developed, such as in dual language programs or developmental bilingual education programs. Additive bilingualism is linked to high self-esteem, increased cognitive flexibility, and higher levels of proficiency in L2 . The opposite of subtractive bilingualism.

**additive model/common underlying proficiency.** Theory that both acquisition of first and second languages can contribute to underlying language proficiency. Experiences with both languages, according to Cummins, promote the development of the proficiency underlying both languages, given adequate motivation and exposure to both, within school or the wider environment. SUP (Separate Underlying Proficiency) approach indicates that no such relationship/synergy exists between L1 and L2 language acquisition.

**adjustment/recovery.** At this stage of acculturation, basic needs are met and a routine has been established. There is a noticeable improvement in transition language skills and cross-cultural interactions.

**advanced fluency.** Your student can understand and perform at grade level in both languages and dialects. He or she functions on academic level with peers and maintains two-way conversation. He or she has a vocabulary beyond 12,000 words and demonstrates decontextualized comprehension. Uses enriched vocabulary

**advanced intermediate fluency.** Your student can communicate thoughts and engage in and produce connected narrative. He or she shows good comprehension and uses expanded vocabulary. They may make complex grammatical errors and functions somewhat on an academic level. They have about a 12,000 receptive & active word vocabulary.

**affective filter.** Associated with Krashen's Monitor Model of second language learning, the affective filter is a metaphor that describes a learner's attitudes that affect the relative success of second language acquisition. Negative feelings such as lack of motivation, lack of self-confidence and learning anxiety act as filters that hinder and obstruct language learning. Krashen has opined that the best acquisition will occur in environments where anxiety is low and defensiveness absent, i.e. in contexts where the "affective filter" is low. Optimal input occurs when the "affective filter" is low. The affective filter is a screen of emotion that can block language acquisition or learning if it keeps the users from being too self-conscious or too embarrassed to take risks during communicative exchanges.

**analogy strategy.** Analogy strategies are a useful means of enhancing acquisition and retention of new materials. In analogy, the learner recalls previously experienced patterns, which are similar to the new items. Analogy is also a very effective elaboration of schema (prior knowledge) especially for culturally and linguistically different students. Teachers can encourage minority students to find analogies between new concepts, materials, experiences, or concepts the students have from their home culture or nation of origin. This is a good technique for language development and language transition as well. This use of analogy can be as simple as identifying similar sounds, similar words or cognates, or as complex as discussing similarities and differences in perceptions, values, or abstract concepts.

**anxiety.** One of the manifestations of culture shock is increased or heightened anxiety. This may be manifested by increased worry, concern, or nervousness in anticipation of new, unknown interactions or events.

**assimilation.** Assimilation is one type of adaptive, acculturative response to changes in our sociocultural environment. It usually occurs over time and over multiple generations. It is manifested by a complete substitution of the new culture and language for the existing culture and language and the elimination of all aspects of the previous culture and language.

**attachment.** This refers to an instructional strategy where the teacher intentionally and overtly connects new learning or new topics to what has already been learned at home and in previous schooling. Always connect learning to prior lessons and knowledge. Make connections between the new content or activity and things that are familiar to the learner, making meaningful attachments through analogies and illustrations between the known and the unknown. This may involve lessons highlighting similarities and differences between the new and the known or compare and contrast activities.

**audio-lingual approach.** Non-communicative approach that involves heavy use of mimicry, imitation and drill. Speech and not writing is emphasized. It is perhaps unfair to associate this approach with B.F. Skinner whose theories would in no way preclude a communicative approach to second language acquisition instruction. A behaviorist approach to language learning, which stems from the belief that the ability to make a sound or use correct grammar is an automatic, unconscious act. Instruction is teacher-centered and makes use of drills and dialogue. Vocabulary and sentence patterns are carefully graded and introduced in a sequence, skills of listening and speaking are introduced before reading and writing, and emphasis is placed on accuracy of pronunciation and grammar. The aim is for the learner to gain an automatic, accurate control of basic sentence structures, sounds, and vocabulary. The approach was very popular in the 1950s and 60s, but its use has declined in favor of the communicative approach

**basic interpersonal communication skills.** Basic interpersonal communication skills (BICS) are those that are cognitively-undemanding and include known ideas, vocabulary and syntax. They are the aspects of communication that are used daily in routine communicative exchanges (e.g., while dressing, eating, bathing, playing, etc.). BICS skills represent the informal aspects of social talk as well as skills that do not require a high degree of cognition (e.g., naming objects and actions, referring to non-existence, disappearance, rejection, and negation, and so forth). Students demonstrating BICS might recognize new combinations of known words or phrases and produce single words or short phrases. When students begin to acquire a second language, they are typically able to develop BICS within 2–3 years. Most importantly, Cummins cautioned that students should not be placed in learning situations in which a second language (L2) is used just because they have adequate L2 BICS. Your student can use the language or dialect in informal or social interpersonal conversations. Acronym for Basic Interpersonal Communication Skills, part of a theory of language proficiency developed by Jim Cummins in 1984, which distinguishes BICS from CALP (Cognitive Academic Language Proficiency). BICS is often referred to as "playground English" or "survival English." It is the basic language ability required for face-to-face communication where linguistic interactions are embedded in a situational context (see context-embedded language). This language, which is highly contextualized and often accompanied by gestures, is relatively undemanding cognitively and relies on the context to aid understanding. BICS is much more easily and quickly acquired than CALP, but is not sufficient to meet the cognitive and linguistic demands of an academic classroom.

**bilingualism.** Put simply, bilingualism is the ability to use two languages. However, defining bilingualism is problematic since individuals with varying bilingual characteristics may be classified as bilingual. There may exist distinctions between ability and use of a language; variation in proficiency across the four language dimensions (listening, speaking, reading and writing); differences in proficiency between the two languages; variation in proficiency due to the use of each language for different functions and purposes; and variation in language proficiency over time. People may become bilingual either by acquiring two languages at the same time in childhood or by learning a second language sometime after acquiring their first language.

**bilingual social and academic fluency.** Your student can perform at grade level in both languages and dialects.

**cloze.** A language assessment technique where you blank out every 5th or so word and have the student replace it while reading. Cloze has been used as a language assessment tool for a long time. It has been touted as a valid integrative test of language proficiency, and holds both problems and promises. You may wish to try it as one of your assessment techniques. Cloze was an early language application of Information Theory.

**code-switching.** One of the manifestations of culture shock and a stage in second language acquisition is code switching. This is apparent as an insertion or substitution of sounds, words, syntax, grammar or phrases from existing language or communication process into new, emerging language or communication process. The term used to describe any switch among languages in the course of a conversation, whether at the level of words, sentences or blocks of speech. Code-switching most often occurs when bilinguals are in the presence of other bilinguals who speak the same languages.

**cognitive academic language learning approach (CALLA).** Instructional approach that provides explicit teaching of learning strategies within academic subject areas. Strategies are divided into three major categories: (1) Metacognitive (planning, self-monitoring, classifying, etc.); (2) Cognitive (note taking, summarizing, making inferences, self-reflection, etc.) and (3) Social-affective (Asking questions, cooperative learning, peer tutoring, etc.).

**cognitive/academic language proficiency.** Cognitive academic language proficiency, or CALP takes much longer that BICS to develop; usually about 5–7 years. CALP skills are those that are necessary for literacy obtainment and academic success. CALP enables students to have academic, analytical conversation and to independently acquire factual information. CALP is used to use information acquired to find relationship, make inferences, and draw conclusions. Your student has acquired enough competence in the language or dialect to solve problems or discuss the content of lessons at some length. CALP is the language ability required for academic achievement in a context-reduced environment. Examples of context-reduced environments include classroom lectures and textbook reading assignments. CALP is distinguished from basic interpersonal communication skills (BICS).

**common underlying proficiency.** Theory that both acquisition of first and second languages can contribute to underlying language proficiency. Experiences with both languages, according to Cummins, promote the development of the proficiency underlying both languages, given adequate motivation and exposure to both, within school or the wider environment. SUP (separate underlying proficiency) approach indicates that no such relationship/synergy exists between L1 and L2 language acquisition.

**communicative approaches.** Teaching approach where negotiation for meaning is critical. The teacher becomes a facilitator. Collaborative learning and peer interaction is important. Students and teacher select and organize curriculum contents.

**communicative competence.** Input + 1/Zone of Proximal Development-Input/instruction that is just above the student's abilities. Instruction that is embedded in a meaningful context, modified (paraphrasing, repetition), collaborative/ interactive and multimodal. You have acquired a level of enough competence in the culture, language, and social interaction of your audience that you can exchange information and instruction comfortably. The ability to interact appropriately with others by knowing what to say, to whom, when, where, and how.

**comprehensible input.** An explanation of language learning, proposed by Krashen, that language acquisition is a result of learners being exposed to language constructs and vocabulary that are slightly beyond their current level. This "input" is made comprehensible to students by creating a context that supports its meaning. Krashen has opined that language acquisition occurs when instruction is provided at a level that is comprehensible to the learner. This can be achieved by modeling, demonstration, physical and visual examples, guided practice, and other strategic instructional practices.

**concurrent translation.** A bilingual teaching approach in which the teacher uses two languages interchangeably during instruction. When not carefully planned, this approach may lead to pedagogically random code-switching which may not meet instructional objectives. In addition, students often learn to tune out the language they do not understand and wait for the information in the language they do understand. A more effective approach, new concurrent approach (NCA), developed by Rodolfo Jacobson, is an approach to bilingual instruction that suggests using a structured form of code-switching for delivery of content instruction. Language switches are carefully planned to meet instructional purposes and concepts are reinforced by being considered and processed in both languages. In addition, all four language abilities (listening, speaking, reading and writing) should be addressed in both languages.

**confusion in locus of control.** Locus of control is one of the manifestations of culture shock. Locus of control may be either internal or external and refers to how the individual ascribes control or responsibility for events. Stating "I failed the test because I did not study hard enough," is an example of internal locus of control. "I failed the test because the teacher or the fates were against me," is an example of external locus of control. Under the stress of culture shock, established patterns of control and responsibility can become confused and the separation of internal and external circumstances no longer clear.

**content-based ESL.** This approach to teaching English as a second language makes use of instructional materials, learning tasks, and classroom techniques from academic content areas as the vehicle for developing language, content, cognitive and study skills. English is used as the medium of instruction.

**context-embedded language**. Communication occurring in a context that offers help to comprehension (e.g. visual clues, gestures, expressions, specific location). Language where there are plenty of shared understandings and where meaning is relatively obvious due to help from the physical or social nature of the conversation.

**context-reduced language.** Language where there are few clues as to the meaning of the communication apart from the words themselves. The language is likely to be abstract. Examples: textbook reading, classroom lecture.

**coping strategy.** This is a problem-solving strategy. The advantage of the coping strategy is that it can be used to assist students from different cultural or linguistic backgrounds to deal with non-academic as well as academic aspects of the learning situation. In addition, this strategy has been found to be effective in cross-cultural situations. The students are taught to confront the problem substantively and not emotionally; engage and initiate action; conceive of a possible solution; request and use assistance; implement their solution; persist in confronting the problem; attempt alternative solutions if the first does not work; and, achieve an outcome.

**critical biliteracy.** Critical biliteracy refers to the ability to read and understand academic or cognitively demanding texts in each language.

**cultural adaptation/culture shock cycle.** Model of what happens when a person is introduced into a new culture and then must return to their home culture. Stages include: (1) pre-departure anxiety; (2) arrival honeymoon; (3) initial culture shock; (4) surface adjustment; (5) mental isolation; (6) return anxiety and (8) re-entry culture shock.

**culture shock.** Culture shock is the common name given to a set of psychological conditions that accompany the process of acculturation. These are normal, typical, temporary side effects of the acculturation process and not manifestations of innate, chronic psychological states. The conditions often reoccur in a cyclical manner, gradually decreasing in intensity over time. Access to intensive transition and adaptation assistance in the school environment can decrease the effects of culture shock for students. The effects may recycle in intensity when the adapting individual is moving frequently among unfamiliar groups of people.

**Cummin's classification of language and content activities.** Divided activities/modes of instruction and learning along two continuums (context embedded/reduced and academic and cognitively demanding /undemanding). Instruction should progress from context embedded/academically non-demanding to context reduced/academically demanding. Teacher should be aware of where his instruction falls and how it is relating to the needs of his students who may be in various stages of language acquisition and development.

**deculturation.** Deculturation is one type of adaptive, acculturative response to changes in our sociocultural environment. Research shows that this psychological response has the most negative long term consequences of adaptive responses. It usually occurs when the individual is removed or isolated from interaction with his or her existing family, community, or cultural group and not provided with adequate transition assistance into the new, unfamiliar environment. Indications of alienation, isolation, and marginalization from home and community are signs that a student is at risk for deculturation particularly when there is limited access to intensive transition and adaptation assistance in the school environment. These students can end up with very maladaptive behavior patterns, substance abuse problems, gang affiliations, and other extremely hazardous learning and behavior profiles.

**developmental bilingual education**. A program that teaches content through two languages and develops both languages with the goal of bilingualism and biliteracy. See also late-exit bilingual education.

**dialogue journal.** A type of writing in which students make entries in a notebook on topics of their choice, to which the teacher responds, modeling effective language but not overtly correcting the student's language.

**dictation.** Dictation has been used as a language assessment tool for a long time. It has been touted as a valid integrative test of language proficiency, and holds both problems and promises. You may wish to try it as one of your assessment techniques

**direct method (Berlitz).** Non-communicative method that involves exclusive use of target/L2 language, uses a step by step progression of material and considers correct translation to be very important.

**disenchantment.** This is the stage of acculturation that occurs as the newcomer encounters problems with being accepted, and with participating in the new environment. The individual becomes overwhelmed with the differences facing him or her and the difficulties of adapting.

**distractibility.** Distractibility is one of the manifestations of culture shock. It can easily be confused with attention deficit disorder or other neurological attention problems. However, the attention and focus problems can be addressed with intensive transition and adaptation assistance in the school environment.

**dual language program/dual immersion.** Also known as two-way immersion or two-way bilingual education, these programs are designed to serve both language minority and language majority students concurrently. Two language groups are put together and instruction is delivered through both languages. For example, in the US, native English-speakers might learn Spanish as a foreign language while continuing to develop their English literacy skills and Spanish-speaking ELLs learn English while developing literacy in Spanish. The goals of the program are for both groups to become biliterate, succeed academically, and develop cross-cultural understanding.

**dynamic indicators of basic early literacy skills (DIBELS)** DIBELS are a set of standardized, individually administered measures of early literacy development. They are designed to be short (one minute) fluency measures used to regularly monitor the development of pre-reading and early reading skills.

**early-exit bilingual education.** A form of transitional bilingual education (TBE) in which children move from bilingual education programs to English-only classes in the first or second year of schooling.

**early production.** Limited social fluency. Your student can speak informally in social settings using basic words, phrases and sentences in the language or dialect. He or she depends heavily on context and produces words in isolation. Verbalizes key words and responds with one/two word answer or short phrases. He or she points, draws, or uses gesture responses and may have mispronunciation and grammar errors.

**embedding.** This refers to a strategy where all instruction in implemented using context rich activities. Embed instruction in concrete, explicit structure or a model, making sure that concrete context is used. This may involve using real objects, models and demonstrations or the use of specific cues and guide structures.

**enculturation.** This begins upon our birth and is where we learn how to interpret the world. It is a process which begins as soon as a caregiver interacts with us at the moment of birth, and includes beliefs, tastes, humor, language, behavior expectations, etc. This diversity makes our mainstream standardized educational processes challenging, as language and culture issues compound the range of diverse abilities we must accommodate within our schools.

**English as a foreign language (EFL).** English as a foreign language (EFL) refers to situations where English is taught to persons living in countries where English is not the medium of instruction in the schools or to international students in the US who intend to return to their home countries. In EFL classes, English is taught as a subject, and exposure to English is typically limited to the classroom setting (e.g., English in Japan).

**English language development (ELD).** English language development (ELD) means instruction designed specifically for English language learners to develop their listening, speaking, reading, and writing skills in English. This type of instruction is also known as "English as a second language" (ESL), "teaching English to speakers of other languages" (TESOL), or "English for speakers of other languages" (ESOL). ELD, ESL, TESOL or ESOL standards are a version of English language arts standards that have been crafted to address the specific developmental stages of students learning English. ELD classes (ala the Freemans) are designed for students with lower levels of English proficiency and less primary language academic development. In ELD classes, the focus is on learning English through content instruction suited to the level of the students' academic background. For this reason, teachers provide first language support whenever possible, especially to help students with key ideas and concepts.

**English language learner.** English Language Learners (ELLs) are students whose first language is not English and who are in the process of learning English. Also see LEP.

**English-only.** An umbrella term that is used to refer to different federal and state legislative initiatives and various national, state, and local organizations, all of which involve the effort to make English the official language of the United States. The initiatives and organizations vary in the degree to which they promote the suppression of non-English languages. The official English movement is spearheaded by two national organizations: U.S. English and English First.

**English plus.** A movement based on the belief that all U.S. residents should have the opportunity to become proficient in English plus one or more other languages.

**English as a second language (ESL).** English as a second language (ESL) is an educational approach in which English language learners are instructed in the use of the English language. Their instruction is based on a special curriculum that typically involves little or no use of the native language, focuses on language (as opposed to content) and is usually taught during specific school periods. For the rest of the school day, students may be placed in mainstream classrooms, an immersion program, or a bilingual education program. Every bilingual education program has an ESL component.

**entry criteria.** A set of criteria for designation of students as English language learners and placement in bilingual education, ESL, or other language support services. Criteria usually include a home language survey and performance on an English language proficiency test.

**evaluation strategy.** Students must learn to evaluate the learning situation to get better at identifying and using appropriate strategies. The skills necessary for an evaluative cognitive learning strategy are: predicting, checking, monitoring, reality testing and coordination, and control of deliberate attempts to study, learn, or solve problems.

**exit criteria.** A set of criteria for ending special services for English language learners and placing them in mainstream English only classes as fluent English speakers. This is usually based on a combination of performance on an English language proficiency test and grades, standardized test scores, or teacher recommendations. In some cases, this redesignation of students may be based on the amount of time they have been in special programs.

**exiting rate.** The rate at which students are moved from programs in which they receive special services as English language learners to mainstream English-only programs. See redesignation rate.

**fascination.** Fascination is sometimes referred to as the "honeymoon" period and refers to the stage of acculturation where the newcomer or beginner finds the new environment or situation interesting and exciting.

**functional approach.** This approach to teaching English as a second language (also referred to as the communicative-based ESL approach or communicative approach) is based on the theory that language is acquired through exposure to meaningful and comprehensible messages, rather than being learned through the formal study of grammar and vocabulary. The goal of communicative-based ESL is communicative competence.

**functional literacy.** You have acquired enough reading and writing ability to accomplish your primary goals and no more.

**gradual exit program.** A bilingual education program in which students gradually transition from native language classes to classes in English. At first, the native language is used for all subjects (except ESL and art, music and physical education). At a later stage, the first language is used for those subjects that are difficult to make comprehensible for those limited in English (social studies and language arts), while English is used in those subjects that are easier to contextualize (math, science). Finally, English is used for all subjects.

**grammar.** A theory or hypothesis, about the organization of language in the mind of speakers of that language—the underlying knowledge that permits understanding and production of language.

**grammar-translation approach.** This is a non-communicative approach that relies heavily on reading and translation, mastery of grammatical rules and accurate writing. The historically dominant method of second language teaching in school. Students were expected to memorize vocabulary and verb declensions, learn rules of grammar and their exceptions, take dictation, and translate written passages. The emphasis was on literacy development rather than the acquisition of oral/aural skills.

**graphic organizers.** Teacher or assistant uses a graph, chart, physical or visual model as a preview/view/review structure for all lesson content, outlining key issues, rehearsing vocabulary, and reviewing related prior knowledge.

**guided practice.** Teacher, student peer or specialist demonstrates what to do to complete a task or how to act or speak in a given situation. The situation is explained in home and community language when possible, and each stage is modeled. Someone who is familiar to the learners comes in and leads them through the situation. This can involve actually physically guiding the learner through the actions required. Students then practice each stage of the interaction with these familiar participants until comfortable with the interaction.

**heritage language.** The language a person regards as their native, home, and/or ancestral language. This covers indigenous languages (e.g. Navajo) and immigrant languages (e.g. Spanish in the U.S.)

**high-stakes assessment.** Any assessment that is used to make a critical decision about a student, such as whether or not a student will move on to the next grade or receive a diploma. School officials using such tests must ensure that students are tested on a curriculum they have had a fair opportunity to learn, so that certain subgroups of students, such as racial and ethnic minority students or students with a disability or limited English proficiency, are not systematically excluded or disadvantaged by the test or the test-taking conditions. Furthermore, high-stakes decisions should not be made on the basis of a single test score, because a single test can only provide a "snapshot" of student achievement and may not accurately reflect an entire year's worth of student progress and achievement.

**home language survey (HLS).** Form completed by parents/guardians that gives information about a student's language background. Must be on file for every LEP student.

**humanistic approach.** Communicative approach that focuses on the whole learner, starts with the individual then expands to group and includes music, art and physical activity.

**immersion approach.** Bilingual program similar to double or two-way program. Sometimes also used to describe a program where L1 students are given academic instruction in a non-native language for enrichment. Approach to teaching language in which the target language is used exclusively to provide all instruction.

**input +1.** Optimal input must be at a level slightly above that of the learner. Krashen labeled this concept "input + 1." To explain this principle, Krashen uses an analogy of an English speaker trying to comprehend Spanish from a radio program. Those of us who have a beginner's ability to speak Spanish and who have listened to a Spanish radio broadcast know how frustrating (and incomprehensible) it can be to try to attend to input that is just too complex and that lacks a visible context from which we can deduce clues.

**integration.** Integration is one type of adaptive, acculturative response to changes in our sociocultural environment. It is characterized by a blending and combining of the known, familiar, language and culture of the family and community with the new language and culture. Some researchers call this bi-cognitive adaptation.

**interdisciplinary approach.** An instructional model where all content areas are combined in thematic units of learning, e.g. The Rainforest, included science, math, reading, writing, art, music, literature, geography, social studies, etc.

**intermediate fluency.** Your student can speak effectively in social settings and can understand and perform many academic tasks in the language or dialect. He or she uses simple but whole sentences and makes some pronunciation & basic grammatical errors but is understood. He or she responds orally and in written form with a limited vocabulary. She or he initiates conversation and questions and shows good comprehension and uses up to 7000 receptive word vocabulary.

**instructional conversations.** Discussion-based lessons geared toward creating opportunities for students' conceptual and linguistic development. They focus on an idea or a student. The teacher encourages expression of students' own ideas, builds upon information students provide and experiences they have had, and guides students to increasingly sophisticated levels of understanding.

**jigsaw.** A specific instructional strategy where a task is broken up into pieces and different parts are given to different groups of students. After completing their portion of the lesson or task, the groups come back together and share their information. In a jigsaw, the whole is only revealed after sharing each part.

**L1.** Primary or heritage language.

**L2.** Secondary language.

**lag time.** The length of time it takes a second language learner to process the information or question directed at them and to form an appropriate response. This lag time may be a considerable span of time.

**language acquisition theory (Krashen and others).** *Acquisition* and *learning* are two separate processes. *Learning* is knowing about a language (formal knowledge). *Acquisition* is the unconscious process that occurs when language is used in real conversation. Language acquisition theory embodies the following hypotheses: Natural Order: Natural progression/order of language development exhibited by infants/young children and/or second language learners (child or adult).Monitor: Learning (as opposed to acquisition) serves to develop a monitor- an error detecting mechanism that scans utterances for accuracy in order to make corrections. As a corollary to the monitor hypothesis, language acquisition instruction should avoid emphasis on error correction and grammar. Such an emphasis might inhibit language acquisition, particularly at the early stages of language development. Input: Input needs to be comprehensible. Affective Filter

**language experience approach.** An approach to literacy development based on the idea that students can learn to write by dictating to the teacher what they already know and can express verbally, and that they can then read that which has been written. Hence, the students' first reading materials come from their own repertoire of language (Richard-Amato, 1996). The language experience approach involves direct transcription of a story or dialog from the students and then using that written language to practice reading. This approach creates authentic text that is at the students' ability level and helps them to make connections between the oral language and the written code.

**language proficiency.** To be proficient in a second language means to effectively communicate or understand thoughts or ideas through the language's grammatical system and its vocabulary, using its sounds or written symbols. Language proficiency is composed of oral (listening and speaking) and written (reading and writing) components as well as academic and non-academic language.

**late-exit bilingual education.** Late-exit programs provide bilingual instruction for three or more years of schooling. Late-exit programs may be transitional or developmental bilingual programs, depending on the goal of the program.

**latency.** The space of time between the end of one person's utterance and the beginning of another speaker's utterance. This length of time is culturally determined and means different things within different cultures and languages/dialects.

**Lau versus Nichols.** Supreme Court case where the Court ruled that, "There is no equality of treatment merely by providing students the same facilities, textbooks, teachers and curriculum, for students who do not understand English are effectively foreclosed from any meaningful education." Also: Lau remedies.

**limited English proficient (LEP).** Limited English proficient (LEP) is the term used by the federal government, most states and local school districts to identify those students who have insufficient English to succeed in English-only classrooms. Increasingly, English language learner (ELL) or English learner (EL) are used in place of LEP.

**maintenance bilingual program.** Bilingual program whose goal is to maintain English learner's native language and culture. Students are encouraged to be proficient in English and their native tongue.

**manipulatives.** Using actual objects or models of objects or items in a lesson in such a way that students handle them and use them as part of learning.

**mental isolation.** This is the stage of acculturation where newcomers experience a kind of "home-sickness." They miss their "home" culture and feel more like an outsider in the new one. They may withdraw from interactions with members of the new sociocultural community.

**metalinguistic skills.** The ability to talk about language, analyze it, think about it, separate it from context, and judge it. Metalinguistic skills, such as phonemic awareness and sound-to-symbol correspondence are regarded as key factors in the development of reading in young children and they may be prerequisite to later language acquisition in reading and writing. Research shows that balanced bilinguals have increased metalinguistic awareness in their abilities to analyze language and their control of internal language processing.

**monolingual.** Your student commonly uses only one language or dialect.

**morphology.** The study of the meaning units in a language (morphemes)

**multiple intelligences.** Theory by Howard Gardner that learners have many ways of learning, e.g. through music, art, thinking, reading, feeling, etc.

**native-language instruction.** The use of a child's home language (generally by a classroom teacher) to provide lessons in academic subjects or to teach reading and other language arts.

**natural approach.** Developed by linguist Stephen Krashen and teacher Tracy Terrell in 1983, the Natural Approach is a methodology for fostering second language acquisition which focuses on teaching communicative skills, both oral and written, and is based on Krashen's theory of language acquisition which assumes that speech emerges in four stages: (1) preproduction (listening and gestures), (2) early production (short phrases), (3) speech emergence (long phrases and sentences), and (4) intermediate fluency (conversation).

**newcomer program.** A program that addresses the specific needs of recent immigrant students, most often at the middle and high school level, especially those with limited or interrupted schooling in their home countries. Major goals of newcomer programs are to acquire beginning English language skills along with core academic skills and to acculturate to the U.S. school system. Some newcomer programs also include primary language development and an orientation to the student's new community.

**one-way program.** Bilingual program where native English speakers do not receive instruction in the native language of the English learners.

**organization strategy.** Recall and retrieval can be enhanced by the use of grouping or cluster strategies. Learning to group or cluster items is an application of the cognitive learning strategy "organization." In organization strategies, students are instructed to follow these steps: Sort the words, items, or information to be recalled into groups sharing some common characteristics; Give these groups distinctive names or labels; Study the items by group, rehearsing the individual and group names; Self-test for recall by group; and, Retrieve item identifications by group.

**phase or stage.** Periods of development that are typically used in discussion of language ability instead of ages to refer to a child's process.

**phonology.** The study of the sound patterns of a language.

**pragmatics.** The general study of how context affects the user's interpretation of language.

**pre-production.** Receptive comprehension. Your student can understand when spoken to, depends on context and has minimal receptive vocabulary. He or she comprehends key words only and points, draws, or uses gesture responses, but may not produce speech. She or he has a 0–500 receptive word vocabulary and may still be adjusting to US/Canadian culture.

**primary Language.** The language of most benefit in learning new and difficult information.

**pull-out ESL.** A program in which LEP students are "pulled out" of regular, mainstream classrooms for special instruction in English as a second language.

**push-in ESL.** In contrast with pull-out ESL instruction, the ESL teacher goes into the regular classrooms to work with English language learners.

**ratcheting.** This refers to a strategy where instruction in implemented expansions and extensions. Extend and build upon what is learned like cogs in a gear mechanism Enrich and expand upon learning. Use skills in L1 to strengthen L2 learning, use skills in L2 to strengthen L1, etc. This may involve teaching specific generalization techniques or using transfer and application strategies.

**realia.** This refers to actual objects or demonstrations of objects or actions. It is an instructional technique for employing manipulatives, pictures of objects, etc. in instruction.

**redesignation.** Generally, the process of changing the English proficiency status of a student from limited English proficient (LEP) to fluent English proficient (FEP). However, within NCLB, such students must be monitored for two years. If they do not continue to make progress in the English-speaking classroom, they can be redesignated back to SEI classes or others providing home language support. Developmental progress of LEP students is reviewed annually. FEP (Fluent English Proficiency) redesignation will occur based on the following criteria: 1) Teacher recommendation 2) SOLOM 3) Oral English Fluency (LAS-O and other assessment tests) 4) Reading/Writing (LAS R/W and other assessment tests) 5) Student writing sample 6) CTBS score of 36 percentile or greater in reading, language and math)

**redesignation rate.** The percentage of students who are reclassified from limited English proficient (LEP) to fluent English proficient each year. The redesignation rate is often used as part of the accountability system for a school or district, although it does not provide valid data on program effectiveness.

**rehearsal strategy.** Rehearsal and other review and retention strategies have been shown to be effective cognitive learning strategies. In rehearsal, students are instructed to practice saying each item aloud and by groups of items. Visual cues and visual imagery also have been shown to enhance retention whether in conjunction with verbal rehearsal or as a form of rehearsal themselves.

**rejection.** Rejection is one type of adaptive, acculturative response to changes in our sociocultural environment. The individual experiencing acculturation may make an intentional choice to reject his or her home language and culture and attempt to use only the new modes of interaction. Rejection can also occur the other direction, i.e. the individual rejects the new language and culture and attempts to only interact within their home language and culture community.

**response fatigue.** One of the manifestations of culture shock is a pattern of response fatigue. The individual is expending a great deal of energy attending to all that is going on, sights, sounds, movements, objects, etc. Without a filter to identify important and critical stimuli from unimportant, the individual must attend to all. This can be exhausting and overwhelming. Response fatigue is often cyclical, i.e. the individual becomes overwhelmed with continual interaction with their environment and 'shuts down' periodically to recover and regain control.

**rubrics.** A structure for organizing criteria; facilitates the monitoring and measuring the completion of a task or lesson or goal.

**scaffolding.** Providing contextual supports for meaning during instruction or assessment, such as visual displays, classified lists, or tables or graphs. Supporting structures or activities that assist a language learner in comprehending and interacting with new information or vocabulary.

**semantics.** The study of meanings of individual words and or larger units such as phrases and sentences.

**sheltered English.** An instructional approach used to make academic instruction in English understandable to English language learners to help them acquire proficiency in English while at the same time achieving in content areas. Sheltered English instruction differs from ESL in that English is not taught as a language with a focus on learning the language. Rather, content knowledge and skills are the goals. In the sheltered classroom, teachers use simplified language, physical activities, visual aids, and the environment to teach vocabulary for concept development in mathematics, science, social studies and other subjects.

**sheltered instruction observation protocol (SIOP).** SIOP is a program for structuring instruction for ELL students. It includes specific steps for teachers to follow in preparing and implementing their lessons.

**silence stage.** This is a common stage in second language acquisition and is also one of the manifestations of culture shock. The individual is spending a lot of energy listening and observing, processing what is occurring before feeling comfortable responding to a situation or interaction.

**silent way.** Communicative approach that makes learner responsible for own learning and makes extensive use of Cuisenaire rods, color-coding and other manipulatives.

**SOLOM (Student Oral Language Observation Matrix).** Rating form with clear rubrics designed to help teachers assess oral language skills of students.

**specially-designed academic instruction in English (SDAIE).** SDAIE classes (ala the Freemans) are for students with intermediate to advanced levels of English proficiency and grade-level academic development in their primary language. SDAIE classes are content classes taught using special techniques to make instruction comprehensible. SDAIE differs from ELD in that the focus is on academic content, not on language development. Students must deal with the content and textbooks that mainstream classes use and SDAIE classes are content classes taught using special techniques to make the instruction comprehensible. In addition, teachers pay special attention to helping students deal with academic texts in English.

**speech emergence.** Intermediate social fluency, and limited academic fluency. Your student uses short phrases and makes many mistakes in grammar. She or he generally responds orally and hears smaller elements of speech. A he or she function on a social level and uses a limited vocabulary (between 1000–6000 receptive vocabulary).

**submersion.** Sink or swim approach to ELD instruction. L2 students are placed in the same classes as L1 students and required to learn as much as they can.

**subtractive bilingualism.** When learning a second language interferes with the learning of a first language. The second language replaces the first language. This is commonly found in children who emigrate to a foreign country when they are young, especially in cases of orphans who are deprived of their first language input. This can be contrasted to additive bilingualism.

**Suggestopedia.** Communicative approach that uses baroque music (in the session phase of a lesson) and stresses a welcoming atmosphere and natural settings. A Suggestopedia lesson may have three phases: (1) presession; (2) session and (3) postsession.

**syntax.** The study of the sentence patterns of a language and rules that govern the correctness of a sentence.

**thematic instruction approach. See interdisciplinary approach**

**threshold theory.** Research on thinking and bilingualism suggests two "thresholds," each a level of language competence in the first or second language that must be passed to reach the next level of competence. The three levels are: limited bilingual, less balanced bilingual (age-appropriate competence in one language) and balanced bilingual (age-appropriate competence in both languages). The Threshold theory, developed by linguist Jim Cummins, helps to explain why language minority children taught only through the second language may fail in school and why children educated in developmental bilingual programs may have a cognitive advantage over monolingual students.

**total physical response (TPR).** Communicative approach where students respond with actions, not words first. Instruction is concrete and can be introductory to reading/writing experiences. A popular and effective way of teaching language developed by James Asher that actively involves the students and focuses on understanding the language rather than speaking it. TPR method asks the students to demonstrate that they understand the new language by responding to a command with an action. At first, the teacher gives the commands and does the actions along with the student. As the student understands the vocabulary, the teacher stops doing the action and has the student do the action alone. Later, the student can give commands to other students or to the teacher.

**transition.** Bilingual program whose goal is to help English learners ultimately adjust to an all- English educational program. May be early-exit ( 2nd grade) or late-exit (6th grade).

**transfer.** One of the fundamentals of bilingual education is that knowledge and skills learned in the native language may be transferred to English. This holds true for content knowledge and concepts as well as language skills, such as orthography and reading strategies. The transfer of skills shortens the developmental progression of these skills in the second language. Language skills that are not used in the first language may need to be explicitly taught in the course of second language development, but content area knowledge does not need to be explicitly retaught as long as the relevant English vocabulary is made available.

**two-way program.** Bilingual program where L2 learners receive L1 instruction and L1 students receive L2 instruction. To be effective program must: a) Allow for development of CALP b) Optimal input in both languages c) Focus on academic subjects d) Integrate the curriculum e) Allow for monolingual instruction for sustained periods f) Have home-school collaboration g) Empower students as active learners. H) Make sufficient use of minority language.

**visualization strategy.** A basic description of the visualization strategy is that students learn to stop and review what they are reading or doing periodically. There are five specific questions that guide them through the application of the steps involved in visualization. An example of visualization that I have used is having my students put small red stop signs at the end of sentences in an assigned reading. As they read through the passage, they stop at each sign and answer questions at each stage of their reading. They create visual images of each stage and connect these images to explain the meaning of what they are reading in words and pictures as they are reading it.

**wait time.** The period of silence that a speaker needs to leave after asking a question or making a comment to a second language learner, to give the new speaker a change to process their response.

**whole language.** Whole language is an overall philosophy to learning, which views language as something that should be taught in its entirety, not broken up into small pieces to be decoded. Some common practices include: project-based learning, language experiences, writing using inventive spelling, and little attention paid to errors.

**withdrawal.** This is a common stage in second language acquisition and is also one of the manifestations of culture shock. The individual is not yet comfortable interacting or responding and withdraws from situations where a response is expected of them.

**zone of proximal development.** A level of development attained when children engage in social behavior. Often abbreviated **ZPD**, is the difference between what a learner can do without help and what he or she can do with help. It is a concept developed by the Soviet psychologist and social constructivist Lev Vygotsky (1896—1934). Vygotsky stated that a child follows an adult's example and gradually develops the ability to do certain tasks without help or assistance. Vygotsky's often-quoted definition of zone of proximal development presents it as the distance between the actual developmental level as determined by independent problem solving and the level of potential development as determined through problem solving under adult guidance, or in collaboration with more capable peers. Vygotsky among other educational professionals believes the role of education to be to provide children with experiences which are in their ZPD, thereby encouraging and advancing their individual learning. Full development of the ZPD depends upon full social interaction. The range of skill that can be developed with adult guidance or peer collaboration exceeds what can be attained alone.

# References

American Association for Employment in Education. (2008). *Educator supply and demand in the United States.* Columbus, OH: Author.

Atkinson, D. R., Morten, G., & Sue, D. W. (1998). *Counseling American minorities* (5th ed.). Boston: McGraw-Hill.

Baca, L. M., & Cervantes, H. T. (2003). *The bilingual special education interface* (4th ed.). New York: Prentice Hall.

Baca, L. M., Fradd, S. H. & Collier, C.(1990) Progress in preparing personnel to meet the needs of the handicapped limited English proficient students: results of a survey in three highly impacted states. *Journal of Educational Issues of Minority Students,* March, (1990).

Baker, C., & Jones, S. P. (1998). *Encyclopedia of bilingualism and bilingual education.* Bristol, UK: Multilingual Matters.

Baker, E. A. (2000). Case-based learning theory: Implications for instructional design. *Journal of Technology and Teacher Education, 8,* 85–95.

Bender, W. N., & Shores, C. (2007). *Response to intervention: A practical guide for every teacher.* Thousand Oaks, CA: Corwin.

Berkeley, S., Bender, W. N., Peaster, L. G., & Saunders, L. (2009). Implementation of response to intervention: A snapshot of progress. *Journal of Learning Disabilities 42,* 85–95.

Berliner, B., & Benard, B. (1995). *More than a message of hope: A district-level policymaker´s guide to understanding resiliency.* San Francisco: Western Regional Center for Drug Free Schools and Communities.

Berry, J. W. (1980). Acculturation as varieties of adaptation. In A. M. Padilla (Ed.), *Acculturation: Theory, models, and some new findings* (pp. 9–25). Boulder, CO: Westview.

Berry, J. W., Kim, U., Power, S., Young, M., & Bajaki, M. (1989). Acculturation attitudes in plural societies. *Applied Psychology: An International Review, 38,* 185–206.

Blumenthal, A. L. (1977). *The process of cognition.* Englewood Cliffs, NJ: Prentice Hall.

Borba, M. (2001). *Building moral intelligence: The seven essential virtues that teach kids to do the right thing.* San Francisco: Jossey-Bass.

Bracken, B. A., & Naglieri, J. A. (2003). Assessing diverse populations with nonverbal tests of general intelligence. In C. R. Reynolds & R. W. Kamphaus (Eds.). *Handbook of psychological and educational assessment of children: Intelligence, aptitude, and achievement* (2nd ed., pp. 243–274). New York: Guilford.

Bradley, R., Danielson, L., & Doolittle, J. (2005). Response to intervention. *Journal of Learning Disabilities, 38,* 485–486.

Brinton, D. M., Snow, M. A., & Wesche, M. B. (2003). *Content-based second language instruction* (Michigan Classics Edition). Ann Arbor: University of Michigan Press.

Bui, Y., Simpson, R., & Alvarado, J. L. (2007, April). *RTI meets multicultural issues in special education.* Paper presented at the annual Council for Exceptional Children conference, Louisville, KY.

Burnham, J. J., Mantero, M., & Hooper, L. M. (2009, January). Experiential training: Connecting school counselors-in-training, English as a second language (ESL) teachers, and ESL students. *Journal of Multicultural Counseling and Development, 37*(1), 2–14.

Chesarek, S. (1981, March). *Cognitive consequences of home or school education in a limited second language: A case study in the Crow Indian bilingual community.* Paper presented at the Language Proficiency Assessment Symposium, Airlie House, VA.

Cohen, D. K., & Hill, H. (2001). *Learning policy: When state education reform works.* New Haven, CT: Yale University Press.

Cole, R. W. (Ed.). (1995). *Educating everybody's children: Diverse teaching strategies for diverse learners.* Alexandria, VA: Association for Supervision and Curriculum Development.

Collier, C. (1985). A comparison of acculturation and education characteristics of referred and nonreferred culturally and linguistically different children. *Dissertation Abstracts International, 46,* 2993A.

Collier, C. (2004a). *Acculturation quick screen.* Ferndale, WA: CrossCultural Developmental Education Services.

Collier, C. (2004b). Developing instructional plans and curriculum for the bilingual special education students. In L. Baca & H. Cervantes (Eds.), *The bilingual special education interface* (4th ed., 214–263). Upper Saddle River, NJ: Pearson.

Collier, C. (2005). *Cognitive learning styles and strategies for diverse learners.* Ferndale, WA: CrossCultural Developmental Education Services.

Collier, C. (2008a). *Handbook for second language acquisition.* Ferndale, WA: CrossCultural Developmental Education Services.

Collier, C. (2008b). *Separating difference from disability* (4th ed.). Ferndale, WA: CrossCultural Developmental Education Services.

Collier, C. (2010). *Acculturation quick screen.* Ferndale, WA: CrossCultural Developmental Education Services.

Council of Chief of State Officers. (1991). *Summary of state practices concerning the assessment of and the data collection about LEP students.* Washington, DC: Author.

Cuellar, I., Arnold, B., & Maldonado, R. (1995). Acculturation rating scale for Mexican Americans II: A revision of the original ARSMA scale. *Hispanic Journal of Behavioral Science, 17,* 275–304.

Cummins, J. (1981). The role of primary language development in promoting educational success for language minority students. In Bilingual Education Office (Ed.), *Schooling and language-minority students: A theoretical framework* (pp. 3–47). Los Angeles: Evaluation, Dissemination and Assessment Center, California State University.

Cummins, J. (1984). *Bilingualism and special education: Issues in assessment and pedagogy.* Avon, UK: Multilingual Matters.

Cummins, J. (1989). *Bilingual education: History, politics, theory, and practice.* Trenton, NJ: Crane Publishing.

Darling-Hammond, L., & Sclan, E. M. (1996). Who teaches and why: Dilemmas of building a profession for the twenty-first century schools. In J. Sikula, T. J. Buttery, & E. Guyton (Eds.), *Handbook of research on teacher education* (pp. 67–101). New York: Simon & Schuster/Macmillan.

Desimone, L., Garet, M., Birman, A., Porter, A., & Yoon, K. (2002). How do district management and implementation strategies relate to the quality of the professional development that districts provide to teachers? *Teachers College Record, 104*(7), 1265–1312.

De Valenzuela, J. (2000, September 3). Una Universidad de Massachusetts crea la primera cátedra mundial de 'spanglish'. *El Pais,* Available from www.elpais.es

DeVries Guth, N., & Stephens Pettengill, S. (2005). *Leading a successful reading program: Administrators and reading specialists working together to make it happen.* Newark, DE: International Reading Association.

Duran, R. P. (1994). *An assessment program for Hispanic students referred for special education testing.* Santa Barbara, CA: University of California, Santa Barbara.

Dyrcia S. v. Board of Education of the City of New York, 79 C. 2562 (1979).

Echevarria, J., & Graves, A. (2006). *Sheltered content instruction: Teaching English language learners with diverse abilities* (3rd ed.). Boston: Allyn & Bacon.

Echevarria, J., Vogt, M. E., & Short, D. J. (2007). *Making content comprehensible for English language learners: The SIOP model.* Boston: Pearson Allyn & Bacon.

Elliot, J. L., & Thurlow, M. L. (2005). *Improving test performance of students with disabilities . . . on district and state assessments* (2nd ed.). Thousand Oaks, CA: Corwin.

Finn, J. D. (1982). Patterns in special education placement as revealed by the OCR surveys. In K. A. Heller, W. H. Holtzmann, & S. Messich (Eds.), *Placing children in special education: A strategy for equity* (pp. 322–381). Washington, DC: National Academy Press.

Fisher, D., & Frey, N. (2004). *Improving adolescent literacy: Strategies at work.* Upper Saddle River, NJ: Pearson.

Ford, D. Y., Grantham, T. C., & Whiting, G. W. (2008). Another look at the achievement gap: Learning from the experiences of gifted Black students. *Urban Education, 43,* 216–239.

García, O. (2005). Positioning heritage languages in the United States. *Modern Language Journal, 89,* 601–605.

Gardner, H. (1993). *Multiple intelligences: The theory in practice.* New York: Basic Books

Gardner, R. W. (1953). Cognitive styles in categorizing behavior. *Journal of Personality, 22,* 214–233.

Garmston, R. (1987). How administrators support peer coaching. *Educational Leadership, 44*(5), 18–28.

Garmston, R. J., Linder, C., & Whitaker, J. (1993). Reflection on cognitive coaching. *Educational Leadership, 51*(2), 57–61.

Gibbons, P. (2002). *Scaffolding language, scaffolding learning: Teaching second language learners in the mainstream classroom.* Portsmouth, NH: Heinemann.

Gonzales, E. (1982). Issues in the assessment of minorities. In H. L. Swanson & B. L. Watson (Eds.), *Educational and psychological assessment of exceptional children: Theories, strategies, and applications* (pp. 375–389). St. Louis, MO: C. V. Mosby.

Gonzalez, N., Moll, L. C., Floyd-Tenery, M., Rivera, A., Rendon, P., Gonzales, R., & Amanti, C. (1993). *Teaching research on funds of knowledge: Learning from households.* Santa Cruz, CA: The National Center for Research on Cultural Diversity and Second Language Learning.

Goodenough, W. H. (1957). Cultural anthropology and linguistics. In P. Garvin (Ed.), *Report of the 7th annual meeting on linguistics and language study: Monograph series on language and linguistics, No. 9* (pp. 167–173). Washington, DC: Georgetown University Press.

Hall, E. T. (1983). *The dance of life.* Garden City, NY: Anchor Press/Doubleday.

Hammill, D. D. (1987). *Assessing the abilities and instructional needs of students.* Austin, TX: Pro-Ed.

Hannaway, J., & Kimball, K. (1997). *Reports on reform from the field: District and state survey results.* Washington, DC: Urban Institute.

Hansen-Thomas, H. (2008). The math initiative in 7th grade science class: How a daily routine results in academic participation by ELLs. In B. K. Richardson & K. Gomez (Eds.), *The work of language in multicultural classrooms: Talking science, writing science* (pp. 377–413). Mahwah, NJ: Lawrence Erlbaum.

Heacox, D. (2002). *Differentiating instruction in the regular classroom: How to reach and teach all learners, grades 3–12.* Minneapolis, MN: Free Spirit.

Heller, K. A., Holtzman, W. H., & Messick, S. (Eds.). (1982). *Placing children in special education: A strategy for equity.* Washington, DC: National Academy Press.

Henry, W. E. (1947). *The thematic apperception technique in the study of culture-personality relations.* Provincetown, MA: The Journal Press.

Hoover, J. J., Baca, L. M., & Klingner, J. J. (2007). *Methods for teaching culturally and linguistically diverse exceptional learners.* Upper Saddle River, NJ: Prentice Hall.

Hughes, C. A., Deshler, D. D., Ruhl, K. L., & Schumaker, J. B. (1993). Test-taking strategy instruction for adolescents with emotional and behavioral disorders. *Journal of Emotional and Behavioral Disorders, 1,* 188–198.

Individuals with Disabilities Education Act, 20 U.S.C. §§ 1400 et seq.

Irvin, J. L., & Rose, E. O. (1995). *Starting early with study skills: A week-by-week guide for elementary students.* Needham Heights, MA: Allyn & Bacon.

Jose P. v. Ambach, 3 EHLR 551:245 (1979).

Joyce, B., & Showers, B. (1982). The coaching of teaching. *Educational Leadership, 40*(1), 4–16.

Juffer, K. A. (1983). Initial development and validation of an instrument to access degree of culture shock adaptation. In R. J. Bransford (Ed.), *Monograph Series, 4* (pp. 136–149). Boulder, CO: University of Colorado, BUENO Center for Multicultural Education.

Kaplan, R. B. (1966). Cultural thought patterns in intercultural education. *Language Learning, 16,* 1–20.

Knapp, M. (2003). Professional development as a policy pathway. *Review of Research in Education, 27,* 109–157.

Kovelman, I., Baker, S. A., & Petitto, L. (2008). Bilingual and monolingual brains compared: A functional magnetic resonance imaging investigation of syntactic processing and possible "neural signature" of bilingualism. *Journal of Cognitive Neuroscience, 20,* 153–169.

Kovelman, I., & Petitto, L. A. (2002). *Bilingual babies' maturational and linguistic milestones as a function of their age of first exposure to two languages.* Published abstracts of the 32nd annual meeting of the Society for Neuroscience. Orlando, FL.

Krashen, S. (1981). *Second language acquisition.* Oxford, UK: Pergamon.

Kurtz, B. E., & Borkowski, J. G. (1984). Children's metacognition: Exploring relations among knowledge, process, and motivational variables. *Journal of Experimental Child Psychology, 37,* 335–354.

Landis, D., Bennett, J. M., & Bennett, M. J. (Eds.). (2004). *Handbook of intercultural training* (3rd ed.). Thousand Oaks, CA: Sage.

Larry P. v. Riles, 793 F.2d 969 (9th Cir. 1979).

Lapp, D., Flood, J., Brock, C., & Fisher, D. (2007). *Teaching reading to every child* (4th ed.). Mahwah, NJ: Lawrence Erlbaum.

Law, B., & Eckes, M. (2000). Assessment and ESL. In R. F. Flippo & D. C. Caverly (Eds.), *Handbook of college reading and study strategy research.* New York: Routledge.

Lebzelter, S., & Nowacek, E. J. (1999). Reading strategies for secondary students with mild disabilities. *Intervention in School and Clinic, 34,* 212–219.

Lessow-Hurley, J. (1991). *A commonsense guide to bilingual education.* Alexandria, VA: Association for Supervision and Curriculum Development.

Lippi-Green, R. (1997). *English with an accent: Language, ideology and discrimination in the United States.* New York: Routledge.

Little, J. W. (1993). Teachers' professional development in a climate of educational reform. *Educational Evaluation and Policy Analysis, 15,* 129–151.

Lowenhaupt, R., & McKinney, S. (2007, April). *Coaching in context: The role of relationships in the work of three literary coaches.* Paper presented at the American Educational Research Association Conference, Chicago, IL.

Magos, K., & Politi, F. (2008). The creative second language lesson. *RELC Journal, 39,* 96–112.

Mathes, P. G., Pollard-Durodola, S. D., Cardenas-Hagan, E., Linan-Thompson, S., & Vaughn, S. (2007). Teaching struggling readers who are native Spanish speakers: What do we know? *Language, Speech, and Hearing Services in Schools, 38,* 260–271.

Mazur, A., & Givens, S. (2004, February). *A survey of BISPED teacher training programs in the U.S. George Washington University.* Paper presented at the 33rd annual conference of the National Association for Bilingual Education, Albuquerque, NM.

McIntyre, E., Kyle, D. W., Chen, C-T., Kraemer, J., & Parr, J. (2009). *Six principles for teaching English language learners in all classrooms.* Thousand Oaks, CA: Corwin.

McNeil, P., & Klink, S. (2004). *School coaching.* Unpublished manuscript.

Minami, M., & Ovando, C. J. (1995). Language issues in multicultural contexts. In J. A. Banks & C. A. McGee Banks (Eds.), *Handbook of research on multicultural education* (pp.427–444). New York: Macmillan.

Moore, D. W., Alvermann, D. E., & Hinchmann, K. A. (Eds.). (2000). *Struggling adolescent readers: A collection of teaching strategies.* Newark, DE: International Reading Association.

National Center for Education Statistics. (1993). *Schools and Staffing in the United States: A Statistical Profile.* NCES 93–146. Washington, DC: U.S. Government Printing Office.

National Center for Education Statistics. (2000). *Schools and staffing survey (SASS): Public school teacher and private school teacher data files, 1999–2000.* Washington DC: Author.

National Research Council. (1997). *Improving schooling for language-minority children: A research agenda.* Washington DC: National Academy Press.

Nessel, D. D., & Dixon, C. N. (2008). *Using the language experience approach with English language learners: Strategies for engaging students and developing literacy.* Thousand Oaks, CA: Corwin.

Neufeld, B., & Roper, D. (2003). *Coaching: A strategy for developing instructional capacity: Promises and practicalities.* Washington, DC: The Aspen Institute Program on Education and Annenberg Institute for School Reform. Available from www.annenberginstitute.org/images/Coaching.pdf

Ogbu, J. U., & Simons, H. D. (1994). Voluntary and involuntary minorities: A cultural-ecological theory of school performance with some implications for education. *Anthropology & Education Quarterly, 29,* 155–188.

O'Malley, J. M., & Valdez-Pierce, L. (1996). *Authentic assessment for English language learners: Practical approaches for teachers.* New York: Addison-Wesley.

Opitz, M. F. (1998). *Flexible grouping in reading: Practical ways to help all students become better readers.* New York: Scholastic.

Ortiz, A. A., & Artiles, A. J. (2010). Meeting the needs of ELLs with disabilities: A linguistically and culturally responsive model. In G. Li, P. A. Edwards, & L. Gunderson (Eds.), *Best practices in ELL instruction* (pp. 247–272). New York: Guilford Press.

Ortiz, A. A., & Maldonado-Colon, E. (1986). Recognizing learning disabilities in bilingual children: How to lessen inappropriate referrals of language minority students to special education. *Journal of Reading, Writing, and Learning Disabilities International, 2,* 43–56.

Ortiz, A. A., & Yates, J. R. (1984). Staffing and the development of individualized education programs for bilingual exceptional students. In L. M. Baca & H. T. Cervantes (Eds.), *The bilingual special education interface* (pp. 187–213). Columbus, OH: Merrill.

Padilla, A. (Ed.). (1980). *Acculturation: Theory, models, and some new findings. American Association for the Advancement of Science, Symposium Series 39.* Boulder, CO: Westview.

Padrón, Y. N., Waxman, H., Brown, A. P., & Powers, R. A. (2000). *Improving classroom instruction and student learning for resilient and non-resilient English language learners.* Research Brief #7: Center for Research on Education, Diversity and Excellence (CREDE). Washington, DC: Center for Applied Linguistics.

Palincsar, A. S. (1986). Metacognitive strategy instruction. *Exceptional Children, 53,* 118–125.

Palincsar, A. S., & Brown, A. L. (1987). Enhancing instructional time through attention to metacognition. *Journal of Learning Disabilities, 20,* 66–75.

Redfield, R., Linton, R., & Herskovits, M. (1936). Memorandum on the study of acculturation. *American Anthropologist, 38,*149–152.

Rogler, L. H., Cortes, D. E., & Malgady, R. G. (1991). Acculturation and mental health status among Hispanics: Convergence and new directions for research. *American Psychologist, 46,* 585–597.

Rueda, R. (1985, June). *A predictive analysis of decision-making with handicapped limited English proficient students.* Paper presented at the Council for Exceptional Children Third Annual Symposium: Hispanic Children and Youth, Denver, CO.

Rueda, R., & Mercer, J. R. (1985, June). *Predictive analysis of decision making with language minority handicapped children.* Paper presented at the BUENO Center's 3rd annual symposium on Bilingual Education, Denver, CO.

Rumbaut, R. G. (2005, June). *A language graveyard? Immigration, generation, and linguistic acculturation in the United States.* Paper presented to the international conference on The Integration of Immigrants: Language and Educational Achievement Social Science Research Center, Berlin, Germany.

Rymes, B., Cahnmann-Taylor, M., & Souto-Manning, M. (2008). Bilingual teachers' performances of power and conflict. *Teaching Education, 19,* 93–107.

Samuels, C. A. (2007, December). Minorities in special education studied by U.S. Panel. *Education Week, 27*(15), 18, 20.

Schnell, J. (1996). *Understanding the shock in culture shock.* Unpublished paper. (ERIC Document Reproduction Service No. ED398616)

Short, J. L., & Porro-Salinas, P. M. (1996, August). *Acculturation, coping and psychological adjustment of Central American immigrants.* Paper presented at annual meeting of the American Psychological Association, Toronto, Canada.

Showers, B. (1985). Teachers coaching teachers. *Educational Leadership, 42*(7), 43–49.

Showers, B., & Joyce, B. (1996). The evolution of peer coaching. *Educational Leadership, 53*(6), 12–16.

Stefanakis, E. H. (1998). Whose judgment counts? Assessing bilingual children, K–3. Portsmouth, NH: Heinemann.

Stein, M. K., & D'Amico, L. (2002). Inquiry at the crossroads of policy and learning: A study of a district-wide literacy initiative. *Teachers College Record, 104*(7), 1313–1344.

Stephens, T. M., Blackhurst, A. E., & Magliocca, L. A. (1982). *Teaching mainstreamed students.* New York: John Wiley.

Strickland, D. S., Ganske, K., & Monroe, J. K. (2002). *Supporting struggling readers and writers: Strategies for classroom intervention 3–6.* Newark, DE: International Reading Association.

Szapocznik, J., & Kurtines, W. (1980). Acculturation, biculturalism and adjustment among Cuban Americans. In A. Padilla (Ed.), *Acculturation: Theory, modes, and some new findings. American Association for the Advancement of Science, Symposium Series 39*, pp. 139–159). Boulder, CO: Westview.

Szapocznik, J., Scopetta, M. A., Kurtines, W., & Aranalde, M. A. (1978). Theory and measurement of acculturation. *Interamerican Journal of Psychology, 12*, 1113–1120.

Taylor, J. E. (2008). Instructional coaching: The state of the art. In M. M. Mangin & S. R. Stoelinga (Eds.), *Effective teacher leadership: Using research to inform and reform.* New York: Teachers College Press.

Thomas, W. P., & Collier, V. (1997). *School effectiveness for language-minority students.* Washington, DC: National Clearinghouse for Bilingual Education.

Thomas, W. P., & Collier, V. (2002). *A national study of school effectiveness for language-minority students' long-term academic achievement.* Santa Cruz, CA: University of California Center for Research, Education, Diversity and Excellence.

Tomlinson, C. A. (1999). *The differentiated classroom: Responding to the needs of all learners.* Alexandria, VA: Association for Supervision and Curriculum Development

Tovani, C. (2000). *I read it, but I don't get it: Comprehension strategies for adolescent readers.* Portland, ME: Stenhouse.

Trudgill, P. (2000). Sociohistorical linguistics and dialect survival: A note on another Nova Scotian exclave. In M. Ljung (Ed.), *Linguistic structure and variation.* Stockholm: Stockholm University Press.

U.S. Census Bureau (2005). *Annual Estimates of the Population by Sex, Race and Hispanic or Latino Origin for the United States.* Retrieved July 3, 2010, from http://www.census.gov/popest/national/asrh/NC-EST2005-srh.html

Vaughn, S., & Linan-Thompson, S. (2007). *Research-based methods of reading instruction for English language learners: Grades K–4.* Alexandria, VA: Association for Supervision and Curriculum Development.

Vygotsky, L. S. (1962). *Thought and language.* Cambridge, MA: MIT Press.

Vygotsky, L. S. (1978). *Mind in society: The development of higher psychological processes.* Cambridge, MA: Harvard University Press.

Wallis, C. (2008, February 13). How to make great teachers. *Time Magazine, 171*(8), 28–34.

Wasik, B. H. (Ed.). (2004). *Handbook of family literacy.* Mahwah, NJ: Lawrence Erlbaum.

Waxman, H. C., & Padrón, Y. N. (2002). Research-based teaching practices that improve the education of English language learners. In L. Minaya-Rowe (Ed.), *Teaching training and effective pedagogy in the context of student diversity* (pp. 3–38). Greenwich, CT: Information Age.

Webster-Stratton, C., & Reid, M. J. (2008). Strengthening social and emotional competence in socioeconomically disadvantaged young children: Preschool and kindergarten school-based curricula. In W. H. Brown, S. L. Odom, & S. R. McConnell (Eds.), *Risk, disability, and intervention* (pp. 185–203). Baltimore, MD: Paul H. Brookes.

Wolpow, R., Johnson, M. M., Hertel, R., & Kincaid, S. O. (2009). *The heart of learning and teaching: Compassion, resiliency, and academic success.* Olympia, WA: Washington State Office of Superintendent of Public Instruction.

Wong Fillmore, L. (1991). When learning a second language means losing the first. *Early Childhood Research Quarterly, 6*, 323–346.

Ysseldyke, J. E., & Algozzine, B. (1982). *Critical issues in special and remedial education.* Boston: Houghton Mifflin.

# Index

**CORWIN**
A SAGE Company

The Corwin logo—a raven striding across an open book—represents the union of courage and learning. Corwin is committed to improving education for all learners by publishing books and other professional development resources for those serving the field of PreK–12 education. By providing practical, hands-on materials, Corwin continues to carry out the promise of its motto: **"Helping Educators Do Their Work Better."**